NOT A SUPER-SAINT

Not A Super-Saint

LIZ HANSFORD

CHRISTINA PRESS
CROWBOROUGH, EAST SUSSEX

First published in Great Britain 1998

British Library Cataloguing Data
A catalogue record for this book is available
from the British Library.

ISBN 1 901387 08 9

Designed and produced by Bookprint Creative Services
P.O. Box 827, BN21 3YJ, England for
CHRISTINA PRESS LTD
Highland House, Aviemore Road
Crowborough, East Sussex, TN6 1QX.
Printed in Great Britain.

To John, Emma, Nathan, Philip and Charis –
more precious than gold.

The love of family shelters like a tree.

Acknowledgements

My thanks to all ministry wives everywhere, many of whom walk wounded, who have shared their pain and their hopes, their fears and their as yet unrealised dreams.

Thanks to the many friends who shared their stories or their special areas of knowledge: in particular Lynda Neilands for her ongoing encouragement and thoughtful comments, Gordon and Beryl Whitehead for keeping me right on all things Anglican, Hugh and Helen Minford (Maltesers will never be the same again!), Barbara Reid for a mouse tale, Lorraine Graham for 'Money, Sex and Power', and Ken Elliott, Derek Smith and David Stark for their suggestions. Most of all my thanks and love to my husband, John, from whom I have learnt much of what I know and who still loves me despite PMS, and my children, Emma, Nathan, Philip and Charis, four very special people, who patiently endured late meals and a mother whose mind was not on earthly things. Your creative screen-saver messages were a lifeline!

Saturday 9th November

I would really like to be normal. Just sort of ordinary and unexceptional instead of Mrs Rev, super-saint, gold star and three stripes for long service to women's meetings.

Wonder if other ministry wives think the same way. They all *seem* so good and gifted and perfect for the job. They're all unearthly creatures with supernatural powers of forgiveness, gigantic though humble spirituality and of course an insatiable desire for deep personal fulfilment through church flower arranging. Why am I different?

Monday to Friday's substitute teaching is the easy stuff: preparing A-level notes on the thematic unity of Shakespeare's problem plays and marking dog-eared batches of indecipherable essays. Sunday, I shift into keeping up appearances mode: smartly dressed smiling sympathiser, public performer, problem-solver to the world, last-minute replacement Sunday school teacher, any port in a storm piano player, tactful listener and maker of egg sandwiches.

Why do I feel like I'm acting a part all the time? The kids feel the same too.

I have a desperate need to be me, whatever that is!
To be an occasional failure without anyone com-
menting. But can I ever be me and still be the Rev's
wife? Must take myself in hand spiritually. Tomorrow
I will try very hard to be real and open to God and not
a hypocrite, and free to worship and focus on God
rather than *them*.

Sunday 10th November

Raised my hands this morning in the worship time –
managed two inches from 'resting-in-lap' position.
Must resist the temptation to look around and see if
anyone else is doing it too. It's so reassuring to know
you're not alone. Peeked. A sort of surreptitious
glance, carefully disguised as 'concerned parent
surveys youth in the gallery to make sure they're
behaving themselves', but managed a panoramic
sweep of almost all potential hand-raisers. Only one
in action; Mavis Gladhope doing the full hanging
from a trapeze bit. It's easy for her – she sits second
row from the back and she's a charismatic import. I
know God looks not on the outward appearance, but
unfortunately man does. Since ours has not been a
hand-raising church, though we are showing the early
signs, I don't want to be a) a source of distraction; b) a
topic of conversation in half a dozen cars on the way
home; c) a 'matters arising' at an office bearers'
meeting. What the Rev's wife does is apparently
public domain material and is 'noticed and commented on', whatever that means.

Trev the Rev's sane voice of reason and wisdom prevails over lunch. 'Do what you think God wants you to do.' Why is that increasingly easier said than done? Why do I get into a tempestuous muddle of right motives and wrong motives and string myself up so much that nothing's clear any more? I want to please God but I'm frightened of people. I mean, there's no problem at a big praise celebration like Spring Onion when you're far away from home and anonymous. And anyway they're all at it and you blend into the crowd of wild, extravagant nose-wallopers – wonder about the incidence of nose-bleeds back in the chalets after a Minehead evening celebration. But at home it's different. And I'm frightened of being different.

Monday 11th November

I am going to make a start on Christmas preparations soon. Plenty of time, though. Feel quite virtuous about planning it well ahead. In fact I would go so far as to say I've really got it under control this year.

Tuesday 12th November

Women's meeting tonight. Speaker Rev Morgan Toogood.

Attendance graph plummets on a male speaker night. This is not at all due to sexism or soaps (well, only for the addicted few). It's just that we all know what they're going to speak on before they begin.

We've had Mary and Martha every year for the last ten years: what they learned, virtues of Mary, vices of Martha, their place as role models. Doesn't it ever occur to the average male that if we all go 'choosing that better part' they'd have a lot fewer hot dinners on tables, no cordon bleu masterpieces at all, a greatly reduced pile of neatly folded, crisply ironed shirts – and they might even have to start a family loo-cleaning rota. 'Oh, sorry dear, just spent two hours in prayer and meditation. By the way, your shirts are in the dirty laundry basket and your dinner's still in Sainsbury's.' Hannah comes a close second: devotion to the Lord, giving up what you love most, patience, worth in God's eyes – only seven times in the last ten-year stretch though. Mitzi, my only sane friend and solace, whispered across the row, 'I'll treat you to coffee in "The Cosy Cup" if it's Mary and Martha.'

'You're on. If it's Hannah, I'll pay.'

Unfortunately this was overheard by women in the row in front who took up the prophetic challenge too. Soon the whole room was hanging in expectation of massed coffee out in 'The Cosy Cup'. (If only men knew what we think about while they're preaching!) Strong favourites were Mary and Martha, with Hannah a close second and the woman at the well and Mary Magdalene trailing. We all know that a lone, male speaker is committing hara-kiri if he breathes the words Proverbs 31 – the perfect wife.

When Rev Toogood announced the reading from Leviticus 12 there were sighs of totally shocked dis-belief and disappointment and a mad scramble to look it up. Was there going to be a fresh word for women of our day, or were we being taken back to the bondage of the Levitical law and no cream buns? It was all about spots and boils and disease-ridden skin. Daisy Mild went pale and was nearly sick at the thought of all that oozing flesh. We couldn't get through the praise songs quickly enough so we could hear what the talk was going to be about. Must've been a nightmare choosing songs to do with skin disease, though I suppose it would have been worse if it had been the next chapter, which is on mildew. As it was we had the song with 'Whiter than the snow' in it, and 'Cleanse me from my sin, Lord'.

We were on the edge of our seats by the time Rev Toogood began. 'I chose a rather unusual reading this evening but I feel it to be important to impart the whole counsel of God, and these middle chapters of Leviticus have been the subject of my daily devotionals in recent times, my meat and drink from the word. I have found them to be not without profit and I wish tonight to share with you one or two thoughts on the phrase "The priest shall examine him", found in verses 3,5,6,7,8, etc. We must allow God to examine us. Indeed, just as Martha was forced to examine her heart and learnt to choose not what is good but what is best, so must we too choose the better way.' There was almost an audible cheer at the thought of what we had been spared in the way of boils and diseases and spreading spots, and massed Saturday morning coffee with cream buns in 'The Cosy Cup' was safe.

Sibyl Sharpe says she is not coming back if we do not end the meetings earlier.

Wednesday 13th November

Felt convicted about my attitude to Rev Toogood and his talk. Maybe I need to think more seriously about Mary and Martha, see them in a new light. It's so easy to dismiss men talking to women about women. A kind of reverse chauvinism sets in, a 'What would you know about it?' attitude that switches off at the mere mention of a female biblical character. Set aside half an hour today to meditate on 'the better part'. Had serious problems concentrating with the sound of the washing machine grinding and thumping its innards against the side of the drum. Thought it was about to bang itself through into the next cupboard or shake itself free from the shackles of pipes and wiring and dance its way into the middle of the floor. Bit like some praise meetings I've been to. That led to thoughts about the plumber, followed by finances necessary for a new washing machine, thence to the state of the bank balance in general, then to what I absolutely must buy before the end of the month, like new trainers for Michael, then to the dirty state of his hockey gear and then back to the washing machine. The human mind in spiritual mode is an amazing thing. Did manage en route to pray for the plumber and his family (now intimately known to us after emergencies too numerous to mention), to pray for long life and health for the washing machine, to ask that there might be an unexpected cheque in the post soon and to consider where I might get the best value in trainers and lament teenagers' unwillingness to wear chain-store models. By this time the half an hour was up. I'm clearly a Martha with an unrenewed mind.

Thursday 14th November

Christmas is definitely not going to get the better of me. I am going to be haunted no longer by the sickeningly successful wife of noble character in Proverbs 31. If she can 'laugh at the days to come' then so can I: after all, I've got a Magimix, Sainsbury's and Marks and Spencer. She didn't have Christmas though. Will make a start this week.

Friday 15th November

'Am I being left behind?' Spiritually I mean. Read an article with this title in *Completely and Totally Renewed* magazine and breathed a huge sigh of relief. I am not alone. There are others out there who wonder if they've missed the boat somehow because they don't raise hands or sing the 'right' songs or do the 'in' things or go to a church where they have 'ministry times'. I feel sort of in between because I'm in an in between sort of church. I do so want to be where God wants me to be and not miss out on anything, but I have a real hang-up about what my body is doing. Wish I didn't have one and I was just spirit. Trev says he's glad not all my wishes come true.

Saturday 16th November

Lay in bed and thought about the magazine article, and about Sunday lunch. I can see the biblical warrant for it – raising hands that is – not Sunday lunch. Though if I didn't produce a Sunday roast and a dessert there would be protest in the camp. When you give them cheese sandwiches they pray pointed things like, 'Thank you Lord for this *manna*. Amen.'

Anyway, if men are to lift up holy hands then it's OK, but it feels so ostentatious. And does it automatically include women? And which way should you hold them, palms facing front and waving, like a kid with two right answers, or sort of cup-shaped with eyes closed, as if you're about to receive a surprise present, or forwards as if you're pushing an invisible object? Raising hands is like doing aerobics with two left feet: you watch everybody else so carefully that you do the whole routine one and a half seconds and two moves behind the rest of the class. You're always bending when you should be stretching. Couldn't relax at the thought of the praise time tomorrow morning. Ended up having nightmares about hands covered in gravy being raised through the middle of Yorkshire puddings.

Sunday 17th November

Still facing personal crisis in worship time. I couldn't believe it! The worship leader, the steady, traditional, sane worship leader has thrown caution to the wind and is doing the full YMCA bit at the front – well, the Y bit anyway. Trouble is, if I do it now they'll think I'm just jumping on the band wagon and copying her and it's not genuinely from the heart. Maybe the best thing to do is only to raise my hands when hers are down and make sure mine are down when hers are up. It felt like an amazingly complicated 'Come Dancing' routine and by the time we'd sung five songs I was exhausted by the amount of concentration required to do the opposite of everything she was doing. The most significant problem with this approach is that I had to keep my hands firmly by my sides for lines like 'We raise you up with our praise' and 'I lift my hands unto your throne', and raise them for 'Immortal invisible, God only wise'.

One thing was achieved. I was concentrating so hard on what the worship leader was doing that I forgot the current hand-height struggle and found myself at an all-time record of almost pew-top level. Feel really confused now. If I'm trying to be the same as everybody else why did I spend a whole praise time trying to be completely different?

Monday 18th November

Are we now a charismatic church? I mean do you have to be a charismatic to raise your hands or does raising them automatically make you one? It's all so confusing. You can always tell what kind of church you're in on holiday by a) the kind of hymn book they have – or don't have (an overhead projector is definitely promising on the charismatic rating scale); b) the instruments at the front – high charismatic rating for at least three guitars and full drum kit plus synthesiser and keyboards; pipe organ with organist and choir is a very bad sign; c) the number of hands raised, amount of clapping and sundry other 'signs' these confusing days. So where are *we* now? We have the overhead projector, we have a worship band – cello, flute, guitar, keyboard but no drum kit – yet! And now we have hand-raising as well as clapping. Have we arrived? And did we want to get there anyway?

Tuesday 19th November

Absolutely must make a start on Christmas. I can't face a last-minute rush like last year. It's dishonouring to the Lord not to prepare for his birthday in good time. Need to talk to Trev about cutting down and removing some of the materialistic trappings. This year I am going to succeed in being calm, orderly and gracious. I am not going to be wrapping Christmas stockings at midnight on Christmas Eve and stuffing the turkey at 1 am. I am going to be Proverbs 31 woman in person!

Elder Ned (affectionately known in our home as Big Ears) called. Sybil Sharpe had phoned him about Tim's 'apparel' on Sunday. His 'raiment was unbefitting for a son of the manse'. She was shocked to see 'various parts of his legs' which were visible through the gashes in his trousers and could not concentrate on the sermon because of them. She has offered her expert patching and darning of holes service – for a modest fee. Tim phoned her before I could stop him. Overheard him apologising that his legs were a distraction to her. Silence at the other end. He explained that the holes were genuine designer holes, intended to be there. Horrors! Heard him saying that she was indeed much holier than him. She seems to have been lost for words. Apparently he only just restrained himself from adding, 'Don't worry, Mrs Sharpe, I don't find your legs a distraction at all.' Elder Ned sat open mouthed. He is of the generation when children were seen and not heard.

Wednesday 20th November

This is it! The big FOUR O. Trev the Rev did a bit of tactless leg-pulling before I'd even got out of bed – something about 'the older woman'. Alice, Tim, Michael and Susannah were unexpectedly cheerful. Romped into bed beside me just like they used to do when they were little. Alice said, 'It's no big deal, Mum. By the way, I've booked you in for a facial.' I was just wondering whether that was good or bad, I mean, is it a special treat or do I look so haggard and old that it's a matter of necessity, when Tim produced a jar of anti-wrinkle cream. Smiled and hugged him, but had to fight a sinking feeling that this really is the beginning of the end. Suddenly remembered that awful joke: 'What's old, grey and wrinkly and belongs to Grandad?' Answer: 'Grandma.' I will definitely use the anti-wrinkle cream – but only in the secret confines of a locked bathroom, and will endeavour not to 'belong' to anyone, except of course God. Was momentarily cheered by Trev producing a curiously shaped gift, all done up with bows and a tangle of curled ribbons. Unwrapped it full of a warm glow of gladness at having such a loving family. It was a walking stick. Sometimes they take things too far. Was very grateful for Susannah and Michael's offering of flowers and a 'Life begins at 40' mug. Just a pity Trev had put a packet of Sanatogen in it.

Thought about all of my life so far and what I have experienced. I am of the generation which wore liberty bodices with dozed rubber buttons, ate sweets called acid drops (which had nothing to do with drugs), actually read from the AV – and I can remember cars with running-boards!

It's hard not to feel depressingly old.

Tried to keep my age quiet at work but Cyril the PE teacher, at least sixty and still full of rippling, bronzed muscles, sidled up to me and murmured, 'Just in your prime, eh?' Felt like a bit of well-hung beef. The fact that I'm a Rev's wife doesn't seem to deter him at all – perhaps the lure of the unattainable has something to do with it. I thanked him politely, with a definite tone of moral superiority, but secretly felt rather glad that as far as he was concerned I might be more in need of a hockey stick than a walking stick.

When I got back from work there was a large white sheet stretched between two bamboo canes in the garden, bearing the unmistakable work of the Hansford clan. It read, 'CONGRATULASHONS MUM! 40 TODAY.' Now the whole neighbourhood knows we have an illiterate in the family.

Slumped over a cup of coffee and wondered what they were planning for tonight. Should I make a meal as usual or is there a secret, surprise outing to a flashy restaurant in store? Or will there be a room full of all my friends somewhere, waiting to cheer as I enter? Tea-time approaching fast. Did a quick defrost job on something which looks the right colour, in an unlabelled plastic box at the bottom of the freezer. Always risky since there is rather a lot of stewed rhubarb, circa summer 1990, looking for a home, down there somewhere. Bad choice. Still, maybe rhubarb has possibilities with a bit of curry powder and a few fridge left-overs.

Did a turn of the kitchen with the walking stick, all hunched up and taking shuffley, granny-like steps. Suddenly realised I was being watched through the window by Alice and Tim. Raised my stick and shook it ferociously at them. 'You're really getting into this, Mum,' Alice said, 'Though I think it would look better if you took your false teeth out.'

Trev arrived home at 6.45 pm with fish and chips. You could have cut the atmosphere with a fish knife. How could he? Not even a touch of the orient from The Peking Palace but a soggy vinegar-laden mass from The Happy Haddock (how a haddock ever found happiness battered and deep fried, in a fish and chip shop, I don't know). Determined to make the best of it, so put on my Laura Ashley dress – wish I had a 'little black number' – wish it were possible to fit into a little black number – some make-up and ear-rings and came down wearing my 'I'm hurt but it doesn't matter since I'm a martyr' smile. Felt like battering and deep frying Trev verbally. Just as I was about to slam the knives and forks as noisily as possible onto the table, Trev appeared with a red rose, a bottle of unimaginably expensive perfume and my coat. Had a wonderful evening at a trendy restaurant while the kids ate fish and chips.

Thursday 21st November

Since this is the start of the rest of my life I am determined to be different. These are my resolutions:

Spiritual
1. I am going to have a quiet time every day, always, without fail, ever, for eternity, till the end of time. I hope.
2. I am going to witness, no matter how awkward and inept I feel.
3. I am going to find my spiritual gift – at last.
4. I am going to work on a positive attitude to the criticisers and attackers in our congregation; I am not going to be afraid of them any more.
5. I am going to be vulnerable and open with at least one other human being.

General
1. I am going to extricate myself from church activities and spend some significant time with my children.
2. I am going to find the time to develop a deeper relationship with Trev.
3. I am going to make Trev find time to develop a deeper relationship with me.
4. I am not going to rush around doing supposedly important but actually trivial things any more.

5. I am going to dye my hair blonde and do something to shock the congregation.
6. I am going to take up an exciting non-ministry-wife hobby like parascending or white water rafting.
7. I am going to buy some non-minister's-wife clothes; I have in mind canary yellow dungarees or something long, black and slinky with a slit. I am going to stop buying sensible, useful Marks and Spencer's navy blue skirts.

Friday 22nd November

Up at 6.30 am to put spiritual resolution one into practice. Trev's claim that I was snoring in prayer is totally untrue. I was meditating and may have been groaning over a deep awareness of sin, the Spirit himself making intercession with groans that words cannot express. It is true that Alice, in a fruitless search for a clean school blouse, fell over my prone body lying next to the bed and thought I must have had an argument with Trev and decided to sleep on the floor, but I assured her that it was merely a position of submissive and abject prostration before the Lord. The fact that Trev mentioned that I had actually fallen into this position, knocking the bedside lamp onto the floor and wakening him with the crash, did not help. Alice said, 'You may as well face it, Mum, you're just not a morning person. You go around like a zombie until at least 8 am.'

Decided to take radical action in the light of this.

Went to bed at 8 pm in readiness for my quiet time tomorrow morning.

Had to get up again at 8.30 pm. I had forgotten that Earnest and Grace, our recently returned missionaries, were coming for supper. They had to be content with very crummy, weeks old, bottom-of-the-tin custard creams and disguised, grated dehydrated cheese on toast. Still, it was probably better than sheep's eyeballs on a bed of yams, which they assure me they're more used to. Was regaled by tales of spiritual missionary giants travelling dusty, pot-holed roads, fighting huge, intestinal parasitic worms (I could see Alice threatening this evening's spaghetti), and all-night prayer vigils against the powers of darkness. They're going to find church life here very dull. Surely I can manage just half an hour in the morning waging spiritual warfare? Struggled up to bed well after midnight, having set all the alarms.

Saturday 23rd November

Forgot it was Saturday. This was a big mistake.

I had set the clock radio downstairs to come on at 6 am on full power, so I'd have to get out of bed to put it off. I must say I didn't realise it was capable of such volume. Then, in thoughtfulness for others, I immediately turned it off and put on 'Wake up O sleeper and rise from the dead and Christ will shine on you'. Very appropriate for the moment, I thought, and with considerate and modest volume for those who had not also chosen the higher path of early morning devotions. The rest of the family were not entirely of one mind on the matter of volume. Personally I thought this had more to do with the thinness of the walls in our house and Graham Kendrick's obvious enthusiasm. Michael thought it was the second coming, Trev thought he had wakened up in Maplin's holiday camp, Susannah arrived downstairs wanting to join in the party and I thought Tim was going to assault me. Everyone went back to bed in a bad temper. Quiet time not particularly quiet. Put on a very gentle, calming worship tape to soothe my nerves. It was most effective.

The fact that I was found asleep next to the cassette recorder two hours later did not go down well.

Sunday 24th November

One of those 'just all right' services this morning: sermon all right, worship all right, prayer all right, but nothing special. Didn't feel 'spoken to' or 'ministered to' or 'touched by the Lord' or connect with anything really. Didn't even feel impressed by the masterly nature of Trev's sermon construction. Just felt I was there like a kind of passive glob in a pew, singing the words on auto-pilot and trying desperately to think the right thoughts, keep concentration on the sermon and look as if I was totally engaged in spiritual progress; kind of eager-eyed, mouth slightly open in anticipation of spiritual food and head tilted to one side a bit in thoughtful pose. Looked round the church: there seemed to be rows of them writing furiously, hanging on every word. Judging by the smiling faces afterwards I was alone in my spiritual stupor. Mavis Gladhope thought we had 'a wonderful time', so was forced to agree enthusiastically. She's the kind of person who finds deep meaning in the announcements. Before I knew it, I was at the centre of a group of Trev-worshipping, sermon-drunk maniacs who were leafing through sheaves of notes and quoting from point 3b on verse 9 and how it had really blessed them, and beaming with the joy of the truth in point 7c from verse 24. Joined in, quoting the marvellous implications of the word 'but' in point 6d. In my experience there's always a good 'but' in any sermon worth its salt. Apparently there wasn't. After everybody searching frantically through their notes and not finding it and discussing the wonders of 'but' anyway, somebody remembered that that was last Sunday's sermon. Felt unutterably depressed. And found out.

Sybil Sharpe phoned to register her disapproval of today's choice of hymns.

Monday 25th November

Blessed, blessed day off. Really needed to get away. We drove miles into the country and went for a good long walk, then to a place for lunch. Trev did the reassuring bit, 'You don't always need to feel blessed or even look blessed, just be yourself.' Why is he always so at ease when I'm so uptight? 'To be honest, I didn't think I preached much of a sermon yesterday. It was one of those off days. But you keep on going, knowing in your mind that it's all true, even if you don't feel it at that particular moment. You can't be on a spiritual high all the time.'

I thought Trev was going to have a seizure when Mavis Gladhope's face appeared over the top of the dividing partition behind me, beaming through her last mouthful of pavlova. Is there no escape from the congregation ever, anywhere, even miles from home, in a secluded café, surrounded by high-backed partitions, on your day off?

'Couldn't help overhearing what you were saying, Pastor. We should always be rejoicing, you know. The word is wonderfully wonderful even when preached by a weak, wanting, frail, failing human vessel like yourself, and even when it *appears* boring and heavy and lifeless and repetitive.'

Scowled and muttered to myself, 'Just like this Sunday,' and, 'How dare you say those things about Trev's sermons!'

'Thank you for those kind words of comfort, Mavis,' said Trev in his warmest pastoral voice.

How can he be so nice when they're so unappreciative?

'Oh no, don't thank me. God has called me to be the voice of encouragement to many. I have spoken to most members of the congregation, in like manner, about your sermons. Lest they should be taken up more with the man than the message. You are, after all, just a tube through whom God pours his word. The Spirit does all the directing,' she beamed.

'Actually "the tube" does quite a bit of preparation, Mavis. He slaves away doing time consuming, behind-the-scenes kind of things like study and reading and rereading and working out helpful illustrations and putting it all together in a memorable way and choosing worship songs to link in and praying and agonising over our needs. The Spirit needs willing workers like Trev, open to his leading.'

Mavis looked pale as I waxed more eloquent in Trev's defence. There's nothing quite like a negative congregational comment to bring a ministry wife to the full height of her rhetorical powers.

'I do think such an amazing gift of encouragement should be used sparingly, Mavis,' said Trev.

She went on undeterred, 'Yes, well, I do realise you are an anointed and gifted and very hard-working tube, a tube mightily used and blessed by the Lord, but nonetheless a tube. And you know, Liz, we are called to a mountain-top walk with the Lord.'

'I believe Liz appreciates the mountains even better because of the occasional valley, Mavis. A loving heavenly Father doesn't want us to pretend. He wants us to be real and absolutely honest. You can't meet someone's need when they're pretending they don't have any needs and don't have any areas of failure and weakness.'

'Yes, yes of course, but we are on the victory side.'

'Sometimes we lose the odd battle, Mavis, and by the way, I think Trev's actually a channel.'

Tuesday 26th November

Yippee! Had an out of the blue, not thinking about it at all, spontaneous urge to raise my hands today.

Thank you, thank you, thank you, Graham Kendrick – and thank you, thank you, thank you, Lord! Unfortunately it was while I was driving, listening to a praise tape. But I made the most of it with my right hand, while changing gear with my left (praising the Lord freely is particularly difficult at corners, without causing danger to oneself and other road users). I think I almost sent the driver of a large Volvo skidding into eternity, though I did not actually see the final outcome – just the look in his eyes.

Managed a sort of energetic, bottom bouncing up and down in the seat movement, with a lurching sway every now and again. It's amazing how restrictive seat belts are when you're trying to praise the Lord freely. I was getting quite carried away by the time I arrived at the next set of traffic lights. The man who drew up next to me was clearly fascinated. I didn't realise at first, so engrossed was I in 'Teach me to dance to the beat of your heart', but I was at the full height of my bounce when I caught his eye. I had to pretend I was straining to reach for the sun-roof control at the top of each bounce, like a frustrated dwarf doing aerobics, and look increasingly worried, as if I was having trouble opening it. A real pity it was absolutely lashing down at the time. Smiled across at him, in pretended relief, when it finally rolled open, and then the lights changed. Totally soaked by the time I got to a place where I could stop safely, but struggled on in praise with 'I'm singin' in the rain, yes Lord. Just singin' in the rain, Amen!'

Trev was very sympathetic about my wet state and

assumed I'd got caught out in the rain. I didn't enlighten him until he discovered that the inside of the car was wet too, plus his sermon notes (which I had tried to dry off and only smudged just a little). Was forced to tell the truth. Alice and Tim laughed themselves silly under the table, muttering things like, 'God poured down showers of blessing on you, Mum. You know, "Reign in me", takes on a whole new meaning now.'

Wednesday 27th November

Read an amazing article entitled 'Mastering Ministry Money' in the action-packed magazine *From Pew to Pulpit*. It gave a list of practical suggestions to help those in full-time ministry make ends meet and keep in a state of humility.

1. During the summer months keep all your orange peel, assuming you can afford oranges, wait for a good dry day (this may not be possible in Ireland or Scotland), place sheets of newspaper on your lawn (preferably the back garden, since you won't want to embarrass the church by letting your non-Christian neighbours know how tight things are) and spread the pieces of peel over the paper to dry. This makes excellent free kindling for winter.

2. Fuel bills are always a problem. Here are some excellent suggestions. You will find that a coal or log-effect fire has two bulbs to provide the red-glow effect; remove one of these. NB Replace this prior to any

church committee meeting held in your home, since it gives the wrong impression.

Turn off the pilot light in your gas cooker, it is a waste of gas and matches are much cheaper. Keep the curtains drawn all day in winter, this keeps the heat in and you will probably be out visiting anyway.

3. Share a dog collar. These, and the shirts which go with them, are expensive specialist items, and we suggest two or three pastors might easily share one. This will only be possible for those of you who are in the non-conformist tradition since you probably only use dog collars for weddings, funerals and hospital visitation. Remember to buy a large enough size for all members of your sharing group and try to get a group of similarly sized pastors together in the first place. In the unlikely event of you all needing the dog collar on the same day, it has been known for such a group of sharers to swap shirts in a car at a pre-arranged meeting place such as a car park; this allows for close fellowship without taking up any valuable church time. Timing can be tricky here, especially if a bride should turn up late and thus delay the arranged exchange time. If all else fails you could use a white polo neck at a pinch.

4. Keeping in touch with world events is important if you want your preaching to be relevant to today's affluent business man and woman; however, daily papers are prohibitively expensive on a regular basis. The ideal solution is to go to your friendly, local news-agent very early in the morning, we suggest 6 am – just before he returns the previous day's unsold papers, and ask for yesterday's papers at half price (some

newsagents may even give them free to needy clergy). This should pose no problems since you should be up for your early morning prayer time by then.

5. We hope to provide encouragement to your help-meet with a few culinary suggestions.

Always bulk out minced steak with porridge oats, we recommend a 50/50 mixture, excellent for the digestion – or so we're told. Potato peelings (well scrubbed) are tasty deep fried. You could try this with all vegetable peelings. Your aim should be to become the mistress of left-overs, though the truly committed and forward-thinking ministry wife, it should be said, will have no left-overs.

NB. You should never expect to receive the left-overs from church suppers. These must go to the needy. It is with sorrow that I report that it is not unknown for a ministry wife to pray for small appetites or even a low attendance at church gatherings, so that she may take home tray-loads of soggy sandwiches as potential packed-lunch material, or even buns and biscuits for her own personal use. What is given to the Lord is his alone, and is not for manse consumption.

6. To eke out the family budget we suggest a little part-time job for your wife. Night work is really best, since most congregations require her to be available during the day for counselling, coffee making and visitation of the elderly, and during the evening for meetings. It has to be said that nurses make the best ministry wives since they can do night duty, but it may be too late to take this into consideration. Another possibility is night-time office cleaning and

even the best qualified ministry wife can learn humility from this servant-hearted task.

7. And a final note for all who live in rectories, manses or other church-provided accommodation. You need not worry about where you will live in retirement; many out-of-condition council houses in undesirable areas are available for a low rent, and anyhow the stresses of pastoral life make the chances of a prolonged retirement extremely unlikely.

Grrrr!

Thursday 28th November

Thought I'd make a start on another of my resolutions today. Considering my abject failure so far with early morning quiet times and my very unhumbled response to the article in *From Pew to Pulpit*, I'd better resign myself to something more secular. Thought I'd go for general resolution number six, to buy some non-ministry wife clothes. Phoned my friend Mitzi for some help.

Saturday is to be the big day for the emergence of the new ministry wife. Mitzi says she is taking me in hand in relation to my total appearance and that she loves a challenge. Felt a little hurt at this but didn't show it, just said, 'Oh,' in a quiet little voice. Apparently I am to be a one-store woman no longer.

It has to be said that Mitzi does have flair with clothes. I have particularly heard the men comment on this. Mitzi also has very long, shapely legs, which I have also heard the men comment on. I'm beginning to wonder if I have chosen the right person to accompany me and give advice. I know I talked about something long, black and slinky with a slit but I'm getting cold feet. I know Mitzi is very spiritually minded but somehow her body doesn't seem to have followed her mind.

Friday 29th November

Mitzi called to pick up the beauty salon vouchers I got for my birthday. She says she needs them for Saturday's plan of action.

I am afraid.

I can imagine myself in one of Mitzi's mini skirts with my hair dyed golden blonde just like hers; or rather, I can't remotely imagine myself in one of Mitzi's mini skirts with my hair dyed golden blonde. Panic. I should have left all this until the beginning of the summer holidays so the new me could have got used to itself before it had to face the congregation. It could have had a private week or two of being someone else without anyone knowing and I would have had time to undo it all if I didn't like it.

Maybe I'm being unfair about Mitzi. I mean, what does a spiritual body look like? Is it more spiritual to be dowdy and slightly behind the times in terms of fashion? Realise here is yet another area of life I haven't even begun to think about Christianly. I simply head off to the local charity shop, assuming if it's cheap it must be godly, or to the nearest chain store at sale times. I now have a collection of sale-price things I don't like, but which I felt very virtuous about buying. Maybe I didn't pray enough that the sale-price things would be in colours that suited me. Maybe God would co-operate if I stopped hiding all the things I fancied at the back of the racks so no one else would buy them before sale time.

Alice said, 'Mum, don't get so uptight about it, just enjoy spending some money on yourself without feeling guilty. Anyway, remember what you said last Sunday to Mavis Gladhope when she was wearing all that new gear?'

'Yes, I can distinctly remember complimenting her,' I said.

'Actually, what you said was, "Mavis, that shade of green just suits you. It's so like the old, well-worn, second-hand, cast-off, out-of-date, cheaper-than-cheap, charity shop skirt that I got on the bargain rail last week." If anything was green, Mum, it was you.'

Faithful are the wounds of a daughter.

Saturday 30th November

Trev says he thinks I made the right choice in Mitzi and he can't wait to see the results. He encouraged me to spend whatever I need to. He must be mad!

We set out at 8.30 am. Mitzi says this is serious business and that we need the whole day. I had never been to a beautician's before today. Mitzi couldn't believe me. Possibly this is a good sign, an indication that I am not as unspiritual as I thought. The facial was great: relaxing and soothing. But Mitzi had arranged for me to have 'The Slender Toning Total Body Wrap Mud Treatment which fights cellulite deposits and removes the grey skin tones of winter'. This involved revealing my whole embarrassingly lumpy self and being wrapped in long lengths of mud-soaked bandages. The entire mummified me was then toned and tortured by a machine which wobbled me around, shaking bits of fat I didn't even know I had. I kept thinking of the question you're supposed to ask yourself in any set of dubious circumstances, 'How would you feel if the Lord came back at this very moment and found you here?' I could only assume that it was extremely unlikely that he would recognise me in my present condition and that it was equally unlikely that he would head straight for 'Unique Physique Beauty Salon'. If he did I think he might have laughed at human folly. The thing I actually feared much more was a member of the church finding me here. I can't wait for my new celestial body, this one's more than enough trouble.

I can only say that I was not amused when the police called us to evacuate the building because of a bomb scare. Other women having innocent treatments like eye-lash tinting and manicures didn't turn a hair, but I had to stand, as unobtrusively as possible, in the middle of the street engulfed in muddy bandages, covered by a none too large, pink satin robe. This was not easy and the fact that Mitzi was doubled up with laughter did not help. Old Albert, the most senior of senior citizens from our church, came by and thought we were doing street drama outreach and that I was Lazarus. He applauded my bandaged squirmings and shouted earnestly, 'Risen, risen! Come and see what Jesus can do!' By this time Mitzi was hiding in a shop doorway, convulsed and disowning me. A small crowd began to gather, all eyes fixed on me. I was cornered. 'Yes, risen indeed!' I shouted. 'Three days in the tomb and then the Lord called me, "Come forth Lazarus," and I came.'

'You should have come first with a fancy dress costume like that,' somebody shouted.

'And you too can come to Jesus, just as you are,' I went on. 'Even dressed in filthy rags like me.'

'Oh, I don't know, that's a nice bit of pink satin,' shouted the heckler.

It was just then that I noticed Tim coming up the street. The only thing I could think of doing was covering my head with the pink towel I was holding, shouting out another 'Risen indeed!' and running up the street at top speed, bandages flying. Thankfully, I don't think Tim recognised me. 'You're amazing,' said Mitzi, when she joined me back in the salon. 'Just think, you achieved three resolutions at once: you witnessed, despite being more awkward and inept than any evangelist I've ever seen, you were changing your ministry wife image at the same time, and I reckon you definitely succeeded in shocking the congregation.'

'Well, maybe the first two,' I conceded. 'But I don't think I shocked old Albert. He really thought it was street outreach.'

'Yes, but I do think you probably shocked Sybil Sharpe. I don't think she'll see you as a meek and mild ministry wife ever again.'

'Sybil Sharpe, our Sybil Sharpe, annihilator with a quick cut of the tongue Sybil Sharpe? You're joking. She wasn't? No, she can't have been.'

'Afraid so, second row from the front, well over to the side.'

Abandoned the rest of the day's plans. I couldn't take any more. Retreated to 'The Cosy Cup' for lunch and then home.

Tim regaled us over tea with tales of some lunatic who was trying to witness in the street dressed up as a mummy. 'It's so embarrassing when Christians do such nerdish things as that in public. It almost makes you ashamed to be one of them.'

I went to bed early and prayed that Mitzi and Sybil and old Albert would hold their tongues or be struck dumb (only temporarily of course), that the Lord would remove the whole incident from their memories or that they would all be too sick to come to church tomorrow. Thought that the chance of God's miraculous intervention on such a scale was extremely unlikely, so prayed that they would all be susceptible to bribery. Could not sleep at all.

Sunday 1st December

Woke early thinking alternately about the possibilities of a miracle and what Mitzi, Sybil and old Albert would be susceptible to in the way of a bribe. Which of these is the more Christian response? I have a notion that bribery is specifically condemned in some obscure Old Testament passage, probably Leviticus or

Numbers, but I'd prefer not to know right now. Maybe if I just drop a hint or two about early senile dementia in my family I'll get sympathy instead of ridicule. A hint wouldn't exactly be lying. Maybe I should confess all and get it over with. Really wish I didn't have a conscience, life would be a lot easier.

Had a brilliant idea: I'll say Satan led me into it. I have heard this said before and it seems to work. I think this would go down particularly well with Sybil, since she seems to have had the very same experience herself on occasion. In fact, if past experience is anything to go by, it actually elevates the person so tempted to the level of super-Christian, fully aware of and sensitive to the powers of darkness and doing battle with them, operating in the heavenly realms, waging spiritual warfare on a daily basis but occasionally losing, normally because other less spiritual Christians are failing to hold up the troops on the front line in prayer. This then produces such guilt in the spiritually insensitive and slothful non-prayers that nobody dares to suggest that there might be anything amiss with the person who seems to have failed. Defeat is made the total responsibility of somebody else. I could become a super-spiritual warrior like Earnest and Grace, overnight!

Had a second brilliant idea. I could say that I'd had a word from the Lord, just like Jeremiah burying his pants in the river or Ezekiel lying on his side for ages and ages. 'God told me to do it' has an awesome prophetic ring to it. I'd be seen as a woman of spiritual stature, willing to take risks for God, counting her own reputation as nothing, enduring the possibility of public humiliation for the cause of Christ, witnessing boldly and without fear in a perverse and wicked generation. This has a more immediate appeal.

The only problem with it is that nobody in our church has 'words from the Lord'. So far God has only spoken to us through Scripture, as far as I'm aware. Half of the congregation would therefore label me as theologically suspect, and the other half who secretly want something more would celebrate this great move of the Spirit among us.

The other problem with both approaches is that they bear no relation to the truth whatsoever.

This is a serious drawback.

If I think these kinds of thoughts does anybody else think them too? Surely I can't be alone in wanting to look better than I am?

Decided to be a noble truth-teller and take the consequences. Prayed that God would stand on the side of truth and uprightness and integrity. And that nobody would laugh at me.

Church was awful. Trev, totally unwittingly (though I suspect the Holy Spirit had something to do with it), preached on 'Truth in the innermost parts and the thought life'. Squirmed through 'What a man thinks so he is'. Judging by this morning's thoughts I've had it.

I am fed up with spiritual failure. Determined to make a clean breast of it, especially to Sybil. Went directly to her after the service and made a full confession. Dealt with making a fool of myself in public, bringing the gospel into disrepute, running away in cowardice at the end. Felt like Peter when he denied the Lord. Almost, in a foolhardy moment of wanting a clean conscience, told her about my earlier thoughts of lying my way out of the whole thing.

'Really dear,' she said in her most super-condescending voice, 'I'm so glad you told me. I will pray for you that the Lord will forgive your foolishness. Actually, I wondered who the Lazarus figure was yesterday. I had inadvertently taken my reading glasses when I went out shopping and I didn't realise it was you. How sweet of you to tell me and make yourself so vulnerable.'

Mitzi took my breath away. When I told her about Sybil she used a number of words I didn't know she knew! Then she marched up to Sybil and told her a thing or two about spiritual integrity, pride, confidentiality and respect for things shared, the goodness of a clean conscience, God's loving acceptance of us all and the dangers of being a Pharisee. Nobody has ever *dared* speak to Sybil like that before.

Even Tim and Alice felt sorry for me at lunch-time, though Tim couldn't resist saying something about me having it all wrapped up. A very traumatic weekend.

Monday 2nd December

I would like a *real* word from the Lord some day, something more direct than the systematic plod of daily devotions that aren't very devoted. A special voice or a deep, certain inner conviction, a word of knowledge or a prophecy would do; something to speak into someone else's life with powerful insight and dramatic spiritual results. Something that couldn't be put down to chance or coincidence or psychological imbalance or being overwrought or premenstrual and tearful. Eliminating all of these is very difficult.

I think I may defect to a fully charismatic church just for one service. In disguise of course.

Tuesday 3rd December

Heard strange noises coming from the bedroom this morning. Found Trev in his pyjamas, jumping up and down, waving his hands in the air and sort of yelping in delight. He looked very happy so I assumed the Spirit had fallen on him Toronto-like. Asked him to lay hands on me and pray for me too. He looked really embarrassed. Apparently he'd just opened the post and found an invitation to be a speaker at Spring Onion. Does this mean he's made it in the evangelical world? Is this the super-spiritual-speaker seal of approval? Anyway I suppose it means we'll all be able to afford to go this year. Just think, maybe I'll get to meet Graham Kendrick and all the other Christian VIPs!

Thought later about where I might go for my charismatic fling and who I would go with. Felt guilty about abandoning what Trev and our own church offer; it seems almost like being unfaithful, especially since he's going to be famous now. Decided to leave it till after Christmas. Will Trev have to become a card-carrying charismatic before Spring Onion?

Wednesday 4th December

Went on a Christmas card search today. This is always difficult. Cards must be biblical and reasonably priced and must also make a contribution to charity. Pastors should not send cards with pictures of robins with party hats, polar bears on ice skates, penguins with wine glasses or Santa Claus clearly inebriated. Unfortunately most bargain packs contain these. Candles are acceptable since they symbolise light, as are winter scenes with trees because they reflect God's creation. Best of all are wise men, shepherds or the manger scene (carefully avoiding those which depict Mary with a halo, since these would be theologically unsound). Ended up with 144 identical cards with squirrels cavorting in the snow. Hope this qualifies under the creation category.

Thursday 5th December

Sybil Sharpe is producing her own Christmas cards this year, which she plans to sell in aid of 'The Sharpe Mission to the Lost and Deluded within the Nominal Church'. Apparently they share the *real* message of Christmas. They are printed on thin beige paper and come with mottled newsprint-quality envelopes. Sybil's husband Derek has produced appropriate line drawings for each card. They bear such uplifting messages as 'The Lord is a refining fire', with Derek's drawing of a roaring fire. Apparently Sybil removed the Christmas stockings and the holly he had added at each side of the fireplace since they made the fire look cosy rather than threatening. The cat at the side of the hearth was permitted to stay since it had a wicked grin. She is not pleased that our church has refused to provide funding for this evangelistic enterprise and so Derek has had to duplicate them in the dark, after hours, at the office where he works, in order to save costs to the Lord.

Sybil has found the addresses of all the bishops of the Church of England and is sending them each a card, together with an invitation to our church carol service. She was not pleased when I mentioned that they might have things with robed choirs and candles and processional hymns on at their own cathedrals that particular evening.

Was forced to buy a pack when she called round selling them this evening. They were twice the price of the squirrels cavorting in the snow!

Friday 6th December

I have a major Christmas battle plan for this weekend.

Tonight: Prepare ingredients for Christmas pudding and soak in alcoholic beverage overnight. (Aforementioned beverage having been purchased by Trev at dead of night, wearing long dark overcoat with upturned collar, with me acting as look-out lest any weaker brothers should be passing by or indeed within the premises.)

Saturday 8.30 am: Make Christmas pudding and put it on to steam.

9.00 am: Take Michael to hockey.

10.00 am: Pick up Michael's new friend from rugby and bring him to our house.

10.30 am: Pick up Michael from hockey.

11.00 am: Make four dozen mince pies and freeze.

12.00: Make lunch for boys and Susannah.

Afternoon: Christmas shopping.

Evening: Iron while watching video.

Midnight – 2.00 am: Mark about 2,000 or so long overdue essays

Saturday 7th December

Slight problem last night with the preparation of the Christmas pudding ingredients; I had forgotten to buy the almonds. All the small, local shops were closed so Trev very nobly went on a search around the filling stations to find some. Trouble was most of them only operate a petrol service after midnight with a pay point through a special, theft-proof window, a bit like some banks. Apparently he did not get off to a good start at the first one when he said he was looking for some nuts. After a little misunderstanding he felt obliged to buy the tin of cashew nuts he was offered. He returned at 1 am, having completed a round trip of over twenty-five miles and visited six petrol stations, and with a very wide selection of nuts indeed – mostly salted and honey roast I might add. For the sake of marital harmony, I restrained myself from making any negative comment on the inappropriateness of these particular nuts for inclusion in a Christmas pudding.

Actually managed a good early start and got into the day with a real zing. Was in top gear by 8.30 am. Dropped Michael off at hockey without breaking the speed limit to get him there on time. Back home to tidy up before setting out for David, Michael's new friend. He seems to be a very timid child. Made him some hot chocolate and sent him into the shower to wash off the rugby mud, while I set off on the hockey collection run. It was only when I returned with Michael that I made the awful discovery: David is not David, or rather he is not Michael's friend David, he is some other David whose mother is probably now going frantic and phoning the police. I have abducted this boy who is now standing in my kitchen, in a towelling robe.

Thought of pleas of insanity in court. Maybe I could put him back in his rugby gear, roll him in mud in the back garden and deposit him at the school playing fields without anyone knowing. No one would ever believe his fantastic tales of abduction with hot chocolate and a shower thrown in! Dismissed this scheme as being unworthy of a Christian. After all, it was an honest mistake. If I tell his parents I am a Rev's wife they are sure to believe me, though maybe the whole incident would bring the gospel into disrepute.

Returned to the rugby ground in fear and trembling.

It could have been worse – David's mother did not actually hit me, she only threatened to, though I do think the words she used would probably be termed verbal assault. I had not experienced verbal assault with swear words before, only the kind you get in church.

Unfortunately, by the time we got home, the Christmas pudding had boiled dry and the plastic basin had melted into the base of the saucepan. Ground my teeth and kicked the cooker in frustration.

Need to talk to God about thinking negative thoughts. How do you know if you're *thinking* swear words? Hope it's not as bad as saying them.

Sunday 8th December

Needed a calm oasis today after yesterday's tension.

I am now behind in the Christmas preparation plan. Should I stay away from church and try to catch up? Told Satan to get behind me.

Worked out an alternative Christmas plan *during* the sermon. Buying a Christmas pudding will not be cheating on 'the perfect wife' standard. Mr Kipling's mince pies will do; if I take the foil off they might look like home-made. I will send gift tokens rather than actual presents to all the far-flung relatives. This is in fact good stewardship since it will save on shopping time, wrapping time and postage costs. I think this is what is called 'being wise in season'. I am convinced God understood my need to get the absolutely essential things ready for Christmas. Trev tells me I had that glazed, transfixed, 'I am somewhere else look' while he was preaching. I *was* somewhere else – Tesco's actually. It's amazing how much he can see from up there.

Louise Bell, one of our newest members, asked if she could speak to me after the evening service tonight. I worked myself into a real state during the afternoon, worrying about what her problem might be; did a crash course in James Dobson, Jay Adams, Larry Crabbe, David Seamands and crammed *The Christian Counsellor's Manual*. Interrupted Trev looking over this evening's sermon with enquiries about Louise and her family, trying to fish for potential problem areas. She appears to be well balanced and normal, but then some of the deepest problems are well hidden and only expert probing brings them to the surface – or so the counselling books said.

Looks like I may have to engage in some deep and sensitive probing tonight. Wounds may need to be opened so that deeper healing can take place. Wish I had even a *little* counselling training, or the gift of knowledge or discernment would do, or some more inside information about Louise from somebody who knows her well. Phoned Karen, who brought Louise to church in the first place, she ought to know. Had to go very delicately, without disclosing that it was Louise I was talking about. Made penetrating yet tactful comments about inner healing and the terrible state of marriage today. I think she thought that *I* was trying to tell *her* something, so brought the conversation to a sudden end.

I'm usually all right when someone expresses need directly to me, without any warning – I just put an arm round them and pray. Then I worry about what I've said afterwards. But when I have advance notice I slide into mega counsellor – inferiority mode. What if I can't answer the problem, find the appropriate biblical text, share memorable words of easily digested wisdom?

Spent three hours writing out suitable references for marital problems (lack of communication, financial difficulties, sexual incompatibility, dealing with unfaithfulness), child rearing (disciplining with love, shaping the will without breaking the spirit, teaching Christian values, teenage sexuality). Think I am reasonably prepared, though ran out of time before I could deal with bereavement, homosexuality, healing of the memories and negative birth experiences. Prayed that none of these would be part of Louise's problem. There does seem to be a lot wrong in the Christian world these days. Wonder if I had a negative birth experience? Can't really remember.

Tried all through the service to see if Louise was tearful; this apparently indicates a less deep-seated problem. This was not easy since she was sitting in the back pew, presumably to avoid anyone seeing her distressed state. Mavis asked if I needed the laying on of hands for the twist in my neck and Mitzi offered some 'relaxing and sensual' massage oil for Trev to apply later to ease my evident tension. Accepted the massage oil. After the end of the service I went unobtrusively to the back pew, put an arm around Louise's shoulder and looked at her with sympathetic concern.

Hoped at least some of the congregation would see what a caring and compassionate pastor's wife I am, without, of course, exposing Louise to any public embarrassment. Indicated that I thought it would be best if we went to a more private place. Escorted her the full length of the church and into Trev's vestry. I could see Mavis Gladhope was impressed and on the way out I managed to mutter to her, 'Do pray for me,' and gave her a meaningful 'I am in a counselling situation of some seriousness' look.

'Right Louise,' I said gently, 'How can I help you?'

She looked very worried. 'Well, I'm not sure I ought to ask now, but Alice did suggest it. It's obviously a very secret thing. I didn't realise quite how secret. It's just that I hadn't done it before and I wanted to get it right, what with my in-laws coming and everything. I mean usually we go to them.'

'The Lord understands your heart, he knows you want to get it right, and I'm sure he'll help you,' I said.

'I suppose I hadn't thought about him helping me in something like this, I thought some practical help from you would be best.'

'Louise, he's always there to help, he'll give the practical wisdom too. Maybe we should pray about it right now. You just share your deepest needs with him, and I'll pray for you after you have told him all about it.'

'Dear Lord,' she prayed, 'Thank you for Liz's wise words to me. Thank you for her amazing example of faith in bringing something like this to you. Thank you that you are so concerned about how to make a Christmas pudding. Please help me as I try to make my Christmas pudding tomorrow. You know that I haven't made one before and that I'd really like a recipe but, as Liz has said, you'll give me all the help I need, even down to the practical details of the recipe. Just show me what to put into it, Lord, and don't let me make any mistakes. And Lord, bless all those making Christmas puddings and getting ready for in-laws in the next few weeks and help them. In Jesus' name, Amen.'

'Dear Father,' I prayed, 'Forgive our foolishness. And now just touch Louise in her need. Guide her and reveal your will to her. Bless her pudding-making. May she make a pudding that brings pleasure to you, Lord. Amen.'

'Sorry if I've put any pressure on you, Liz. It was only when you took me into the vestry that I realised how secret your recipe was. It was just that Alice said you had an amazing recipe for Christmas pudding using honey-roast cashew nuts, with a separate, rich, dark layer at the bottom, and I thought that would make it extra special.'

'Don't give it a second thought, Louise. In fact I'd be happy to share that particular recipe with you, but please, please, don't mention it, especially to Mavis Gladhope.'

I will kill Alice when she gets in tonight.

Monday 9th December

Christmas preparations are now seriously behind schedule. Trev volunteered to come Christmas shopping with me today. He has heard me panicking about the number of shopping days left until Christmas and thinks a load shared is a load lightened. Personally, I think a load shared is a load of trouble in this case. I don't mind someone doing the carrying but choosing a dozen gifts together may involve some serious negotiation and significant submission.

A pity we didn't think of praying before we set out. The major public disagreement we had in the middle of Marks and Spencer's would then have been avoided.

I am sure there is a great deal to be said for toiletries for all the ladies of our acquaintance and Christian books for all the men, but it does seem more than a little sexist. When I reminded Trev that women could read too he said he preferred them to smell nice. I did not take this as the bantering, flirtatious comment he says it was intended to be.

We retreated to the Christian bookshop, where we were obliged to smile at each other. I have chosen Christian books for all the *female* members of our family, which I am sure they will benefit from greatly: *The Typology of Scripture* for Aunt Florrie, *The Gospel Mystery of Sanctification* for Aunt Margaret and *God in the Wasteland: the Reality of Truth in a World of Fading Dream* for my cousin who is not yet a Christian but who I am sure will be after reading this. Trev chose Adrian Plass for all the men. I think I have made my point.

Trev spoke to the manager of the Christian bookshop about an exchange or refund policy after Christmas. Oh, husband of little faith.

He says he's glad he married a woman of spirit and that life will never be dull. I was not quite sure how to take this.

Note by the phone when we got home to say that my sister Anne would like a goat for Christmas. Confirmed with Michael that I had read the message correctly. Apparently her daughter, April, phoned to make the suggestion. I know she is into jam-making and stencilling and all things creative but this is a new step. A goat may be hard to find.

Also a message from the Evangelical Alliance – something about a women's body. Returned the call to see if they wanted me to be a conference speaker or maybe serve on a committee. The answering machine was on, so will have to wait to hear about any big ministry opportunity.

Tuesday 10th December

Started making urgent enquiries about a goat. Looks hopeful. A friend of a friend at work knows somebody who sells kids, so I have arranged to collect one on Saturday afternoon. It is quite reasonably priced. I had no idea how much a goat cost. If we ever leave ministry, self-sufficiency may be an option. Trev did not seem to like the idea, he thinks the sheep he currently has are more than enough trouble. Had to calm Susannah down. She overheard me on the phone talking about how much kids cost and thought we might be buying another child. In my opinion four plus Trev is a quiver-full!

Wednesday 11th December

Outreach carol singing around the church neighbourhood tonight. Rather a motley crew turned up, the willing but tuneless. The street-lamp lighting was not as adequate as we had thought and there appeared to be insufficient torches. Not only that, but the Bethlehem Carol Sheets which we were using were circa 1973 and had been so folded, rained on, snowed on and smeared with hamburger relish on at least one occasion (1986, after the youth fellowship Big Mac and fries outreach), that they were fairly indecipherable. But as our leader said, we knew all the words. It's just a pity we didn't all remember the verses coming in the same order. After verse one, over which there was general agreement, it was really every man for himself.

It's amazing how one or two strong personalities can take over on such an occasion of good will. I hadn't realised just how loud Sam Priddle and Derek Sharpe could sing, though perhaps sing wasn't quite the right word. Apparently Sam has been quenching the gift of yodelling for a long time, and Derek is a closet counter-tenor. It's wonderful how the Lord has equipped the saints for all manner of good works. Derek had also equipped himself with castanets borrowed from the toddlers' toy box. I think it could safely be said that the 'Come and worship' bit in 'Angels from the realms of glory' will never sound the same again. Certainly more folk appeared at their windows and front doors than had ever happened before at an outreach carol singing event. I'm not sure whether this was good or bad.

By the time we had got to a thunderous and most unusual version of 'Silent Night', with Derek counter-tenoring verse two while Sam yodelled verse three, the rest of us were in loud conversation with people at their doors, trying to draw attention away from the public display of the church harmonious. Two middle-aged, red-nosed men wearing knitted, woolly bobble hats and vying for carol singing leadership make an interesting sight. Both clearly failed the 'each esteeming others better than yourself' test.

The mounting tension was lightened by the arrival of a couple of drunks. I think Sybil Sharpe's support-ive descant in the 'Sing choirs of angels' verse may have suggested to them that someone was in urgent need of medical attention. It's amazing what agents the Lord uses to bring about peace among the saints. I did hear Mavis Gladhope speculate as to whether they might be angels sent with messages of good will to all men. If so they were very heavily disguised. They led us in a few verses of 'Jingle Bells' and 'Walking in a Winter Wonderland' which proved to be highly reconciliatory. Funny how it suddenly didn't seem to matter at all that we didn't even know half the words, let alone get them in exactly the right order. People started enjoying themselves and smiling. Sometimes it's very hard being a Christian and having to get everything right. I know we're bound to be happier but sometimes it doesn't feel much like it. This worries me. Non-Christians, of course, are allowed to relax and have fun a lot more, while Christians, and especially people in ministry, mustn't ever just have fun. I know this will all be made up for in heaven, but I would quite like a little taste of it now. Do other Christians get tired of trying so hard?

Back at the church hall afterwards, Mavis was heard asking for the gift of interpretation, so the tongues the 'angels' were speaking in could bring enlightenment to us all.

Thursday 12th December

Derek Sharpe phoned to complain about a sore right hand. He suggested we buy a drum kit for next year.

Sybil Sharpe phoned to see if Derek had phoned. I think she may be considering tagging him. She suggested that he be put in charge of carol singing next year since 'the Lord has clearly blessed us as a couple with musical talent and has given Derek an obvious gift of leadership'. Thank goodness the Lord has given Trev the gift of tact.

Friday 13th December

Mitzi says I absolutely must have my new look in time for the festive season. We are to make a second attempt tomorrow. She makes it sound like climbing Everest.

Arrival of the first congregational tin of biscuits.

Saturday 14th December

Spent more than two hours in 'Curl up and Dye', having 'low copper lights in subtle autumn hints' done. Feel about as subtle as Cilla Black. Wonder if *I* could curl up and hide instead of going to church tomorrow. The stylist said my pale skin tones needed a warm glow. Personally I think my pale skin tones would benefit more from a fortnight's package holiday somewhere hot and sunny rather than last year's month under canvas in the rain.

Went to the kind of clothes shops that I always avoid: the young and trendy kind with communal changing rooms and the up-market kind where there's only one or two of everything instead of whole rows full in five safe seasonal colours and six generous sizes.

Mitzi said my taste was far too conservative, so I was to let her select some things and try them on without prejudice. Had to tell her what my real size was. Felt totally exposed, especially when she said, 'My word, you've done a good camouflage job!'

Apparently I'm not made in the sizes clothes come in; seems I've got my own waist and somebody else's hips. This did not do my fading confidence any good. I know Christians should be humble, but I've spent such a long time working biblically on my self-esteem that it seemed a shame to blitz it all in one dress shop. I know I wanted a new image but I was hoping Mitzi would find *something* positive to say about the old one. It's all I've got. Reassured myself that the real me is underneath the clothes and beyond the body, though I know that needs a lot of working on too. Held on to the fact that the Lord loves me as I am. I suppose he'd like a few spiritual modifications though.

I could not believe what Mitzi expected me to wear! Though I must say I felt marvellous when I got it all on. Am not sure that what I am feeling is godly. A lacy top seemed a bit *risqué*, but she wouldn't let me wear my ageing, grey thermal vest under it. I now have a new satin camisole beneath to protect my modesty. We eventually found a long straight black velvet skirt to fit me, with only a moderately-sized slit. Mitzi chose a very large pair of shimmering, dangly ear-rings and high-heeled black patent shoes for me. Apparently this is my evening wear. I have never had evening wear before, apart from cosy tartan pyjamas and a nice warm dressing-gown. When I told Mitzi this she said I was a hopeless case. I cannot imagine wearing the new outfit to the Senior Citizens' Christmas party and the Women's Fellowship dinner, but I suppose I'll have to since these are the only evening events I go to. Do these count or do I need to expand my social activities? I am now very worried that I am *of* the world as well as in it.

Mitzi thinks I need something trendy for everyday wear. She made me try on some Levi jeans and then a short skirt. I did not want to fall out with Mitzi but I do not feel comfortable with my knees exposed. Am really concerned about how short a skirt can be and still be a Christian skirt. And as for the jeans, Mitzi says I should be prepared to put up with a bit of dis-comfort to look good. When I said that I didn't want to be conformed to the world, and anyway my body wasn't conformed to the shape of the jeans, she said that I should at least *try* to think twentieth century and that I was taking a stand for vicars' and pastors' wives everywhere. I think it will be a stand; with the jeans on any other position is physically impossible.

Felt much more at home and considerably less conspicuous being my middle-aged, Marks and Spencer self. I will have to think differently about myself, get my mind to believe that I'm trendy and sophisticated; working on the outside appearance only makes me feel like two different people.

Mitzi made me wear the evening gear on the way home. I think she was afraid I'd take it back if I hadn't taken the labels off and worn it.

Remembered I had to pick the goat up this afternoon. The only way I could think of managing him was to push him into the back of the estate car and tie him up. Mitzi helped *most* reluctantly. Prayed hard that he wouldn't *do* anything in the car. Had real difficulty manoeuvering him out of the car and into the garden wearing my tight black velvet skirt and high heels; was more in need of welly boots and dungarees.

Trev came out to see who the strange woman in the garden was. All he could say was, 'Wow.' I may persevere with the evening wear and the jeans.

Sunday 15th December

Quiet Sunday. Though Sybil Sharpe called round and caught me with *The Antiques Roadshow* on and a hearty pile of exam-marking in front of me. She gave me a real fright when I saw her face pressed up to the window where the curtains don't quite meet in the middle. She expressed concern that I was not at the evening service supporting my husband. And anyhow, watching TV on the Lord's day is not 'the kind of behaviour one would expect of a Rev's wife'. How does she manage to smile and yet look so condescending and disappointed and superior all at the same time? If it had been *Songs of Praise* then there might have been a measure of understanding but *The Antiques Roadshow* apparently induces covetousness and a worldly spirit. Wondered how she knew if she 'never watched such programmes'. She had hoped that my mind might be on higher things. It was. I was praying inwardly that Tim would turn down the volume of 'What will people say when they hear that I'm a Jesus Freak?' which was pounding down from upstairs. I was thinking, 'What will people say when they hear the manse was full of wordly TV and loud teenage music on a Sunday evening?' as they are now bound to. I don't think Sybil understands the concept of Christian rock, she's sort of stuck somewhere between George Beverley Shea and Pat Boone. It did not help when Tim bounded downstairs and greeted her with, 'Hi there Sybil babe! Got my legs totally covered.' She is not into understanding the younger generation.

Monday 16th December

Went to buy Trev his present today. Couldn't decide between something he needs, like new shoes, something he would enjoy, like classical CDs, or something that would do him good, like membership of the local health club. Should I be praying about this sort of thing or just using my common sense?

If I let him wear his old worn shoes to the mid-week meeting and on pastoral visitation then maybe some kind parishioner will 'just happen' to notice his need when he sits down and crosses his legs (as long as he holds his foot up high enough for them to see the worn-out soles) and provide the money to buy new ones. That would narrow the choice down to two. Though if I pay for the health club membership then they'll all think we're wealthy and aren't spending money wisely and then nobody'll do anything about the shoes or the 'keep him humble' salary or anything else for that matter. Came home with two CDs and a box of Grecian 2000 cover grey hair dye for Trev and a teapot for my mother. Is this mean or wise? And if God wants to do abundantly more than all we ask or think should I step out in faith or wait for God to do the abundant bit first? Am I showing a lack of trust?

Tuesday 17th December

Saw Sybil Sharpe in the supermarket. Couldn't handle another earful so hid behind the tins of Christmas biscuits. Had to do all my shopping very carefully, peeping round the end of each aisle before turning into it. Had to reverse rapidly with an unwieldly trolley several times and nearly got caught beside the coffee, having another crisis of conscience over whether I ought to buy the more expensive 'treat the third world fairly' kind or the money-saving, own-label brand. Is hiding from church members deceitful, pragmatic or wise? Life is full of seemingly unanswerable questions.

Wednesday 18th December

Evangelistic meeting planned for Christmas Eve. A 'Bone and stuff your turkey night', with practical demonstration from an expert Christian turkey boner, in Pris Priddle's house. This is by special invitation and we are each to bring 'someone'. Sybil Sharpe says we should pray for spiritually-ready contacts. Makes us sound like a bunch of mediums trying to reach the other side, which I suppose is what we're doing, only before they're dead. Need to pray about who I will bring. Spiritually-ready contacts and oven-ready turkeys is an interesting combination. Second Christmas gift-wrapped tin of biscuits arrived from a church member today.

Thursday 19th December

Unexpectedly saw my neighbour first thing this morning when I was bringing in the milk. This is unusual. It must be a sign that I'm meant to invite her. Hesitated because I was wearing my dressing-gown and felt embarrassed, though called out a friendly, 'Hello.' Making contact in this informal kind of situation is important. If I could do something for her then I would have won the right to ask her.

The goat is enjoying our garden, especially the edible bits of it. What do you feed a goat after he has eaten all the available grass?

Pris phoned to ask if I had 'made any contacts'. She didn't laugh when I said I hadn't had time to reach the other side yet.

Friday 20th December

Lots of cards arriving. Judging from my morning coffee call in the rectory we are doing rather well in the 'Who appreciates their minister most at Christmas' stakes. We have six 'To Our Beloved Pastor' cards and five of the individually chosen with elaborate gold trim and meaningful text, not out of a box or packet variety. When Gwen, the rector's wife, was out making the coffee I noticed that they had only two 'Beloved Pastors' and three specially purchased with embossed edges, though I didn't quite manage to complete the whole room in time. Very reassured. It's so nice to know one is appreciated.

Noticed that Priscilla Priddle has sent the rector a card, not that I actually looked inside *too* many of them. Is she planning on leaving us? Need to tell Trev to make a soothing, we really appreciate you, is everything all right kind of visit. Wish ministry didn't have to be so reactive. Dropped in a comment about Sam's amazing gift of yodelling – hope that will put them off making the Priddles too welcome in Saint Michael's.

Two more tins of congregational biscuits arrived today.

Saturday 21st December

Last major shopping trip. Touch and go as to whether I'll be ready for Christmas in time. Prayed that I'd see my neighbour again this morning. Didn't, despite going out to collect the milk bottles one at a time. Maybe I should ask someone else.

More tins of biscuits from church folk this evening.

Wesley Tweed, who is in his early thirties, pink-faced and eager, called with Christmas greetings – but no biscuits. He sat for a long time on our sofa, just nodding his head sagely and smiling. Occasionally he muttered, 'It's all in the Lord's hands.' Obliged to reply, 'Yes indeed, Wesley,' at intervals. Maybe this will become clear later.

Thankfully, Ned, our elder, appeared and joined him on the sofa. Wesley went on nodding and muttering. Ned was compelled to take on my listening role. It's good for an elder to experience manse life in the raw like this, from time to time.

Tim wanted to know what Noddy and Big Ears wanted. Some day he will get us into serious trouble.

Sunday 22nd December

Evening 'Carols by Candlelight' service. One of my favourites of the year but always fraught with tension over whether the candles will get to the greenery and pine cones and go up in flames before Trev has announced the last carol. It was quite a nail-biting finish this time. Wish somebody else would worry about such things.

Our whole family sang 'Who is he in yonder stall?' together. Alice, Tim, Michael and Susannah sang the question bits and Trev and I sang the answer bits. The fact that we are not exactly the Von Trapp family didn't seem to matter. Could see the congregation wiping away the odd tear. Maybe we are doing the occasional thing right!

Still nobody to ask to the turkey-boning evening; I am getting desperate.

Deluge of biscuits this evening. Great Wall of China made of biscuit tins now forming around the Christmas tree.

Monday 23rd December

Prayed extra hard before collecting the milk bottles this morning. Didn't work.

Phoned the goat lady to ask what goats eat and how to decorate a goat for Christmas; I mean, if I tie a ribbon round his neck will he object and could I put tinsel on his feet without him eating it and if he ate it would it do him any harm? She laughed and said it was best not to stuff him, and boning and cranberry sauce were out of the question. Couldn't believe it! When I said I was actually going to a turkey-boning and stuffing evening tomorrow she said she'd always wanted to know how to do that and could she possibly come. Thank you, thank you Lord! But why do you mostly seem to do something different from what I expect? It really does create anxiety. Trev asked if I'd ever heard of faith and praying according to God's will. Trouble with that is I can't stand all the waiting and uncertainty; I'm the kind of person who digs bulbs up to see if they've started growing yet. Why can't God just do things faster – and preferably in an anticipated way?

Christmas tree now inaccessible due to congregational gifts of biscuits. Anticipating long counselling sessions with plenty of chocolate biscuits in the New Year.

Tuesday 24th December

Turkey boning tonight. Slight panic. Despite the ultimate Christmas success plan I had forgotten to order a turkey! Had to buy a supermarket one instead of a specially ordered, fresh from the country one – still a turkey's a turkey when all's said and done.

The lure of having no abandoned turkey carcass on Christmas evening, waiting to be sliced, portioned, frozen and resurrected at a later date in disguise was enough to draw a crowd. Twelve of us in all, six Christians and six 'contacts', who were, of course, unaware that they were 'contacts'. They think they're all friends. Strange how it never dawns on them that they're potential trophies of grace and mega-spiritual brownie points for the one who brought them, with extra bonus points if they should be converted.

When you're up to your elbows in turkey flesh and innards the conversation doesn't always turn naturally to the Lord. Tried the 'Christmas really has lost its meaning' line but didn't have the courage to push it over the line to goal, so to speak. You could almost hear the hum of Christian minds working overtime trying to think of the ideal evangelistic opening line. Couldn't believe it when Mavis Gladhope said, 'This really is a high salmonella risk area.' A few uncertain laughs and a few worried looks as they anticipated the possibilities. 'But you know, the Lord heals all our diseases.' I was scared stiff, as the religious semi-professional, that I'd be expected to provide a full explanation as to why the Lord clearly *doesn't* heal all our diseases. I know the 'official explanation' but somehow it's only convincing once you're *in*. Fled hurriedly to the loo in fear of an own goal. Just got back in time to hear Mavis have a second shot at subtle and indirect witness as she looked around at the wastes of turkey flesh. 'It was when we were in such a mess that Christ died for us.' You can always sense Christian desperation. Three needed the loo at the same time, two volunteered to make coffee and one thought she heard the door bell ring. Stunned silence when Val, the goat lady, said if she was honest she supposed she was in a mess. Did we think God could really help? A few shared how God had touched their lives and made a real difference. Val was genuinely interested. She's coming to church tomorrow. God you're alive and you're working! Was forced to be honest about *her* asking *me* if she could come, noble but truthful sacrifice of thousands of Christian brownie points. Just had a thought; perhaps I'm laying up treasure in heaven.

Finished gift-wrapping at 1 am. All is well with the world.

Wednesday 25th December

Wonderful Christmas morning service (resisted the temptation to show Val off). Wonderful lunch. Wonderful family. Only blight of the day was the goat.

Took Anne out to the garden, with eyes closed, to meet her gift. She gave what can only be described as a little shriek. Initially I thought this was sheer delight that someone had gone to the trouble of buying her exactly what she wanted. When she backed away, grabbed Alice's hand and refused to touch the blessed thing, I realised this might not be quite the case.

We are now lumbered with a goat. Anne has refused to take it home; she says she can't bear its little tufty white beard. Life with Trev and *five* kids is unimaginable.

Trev had to restrain me from 'laying hands' on Michael. He retreated to his bedroom when I told him that if only he had spent just the odd moment, once every six months, in alternate years, with half a brain attached, on basic French spelling and pronunciation, and if he had just the minimum amount of common sense to establish that he was human, he might not have written, 'ANNE GOAT EA WOMEN'S BODY' but just possibly have recorded the phone message correctly. Apparently Anne actually wanted some

Gaultier perfume in a bottle shaped like a woman's body. Felt like crying. There *is* no women's ministry opportunity with the Evangelical Alliance, just a rotten, smelly, non-productive white goat eating our garden up. And I'll have to go and buy Anne the rotten, smelly, probably wildly expensive perfume into the bargain. Had to struggle *very* hard with my Christian witness for the rest of the day and tell lies about how it was no problem and how delighted I'd be to get her the perfume she really wanted. Even had to smile as I said it, since it was Christmas Day.

Recovered by tea-time and apologised to Michael for over-reacting. Anne apologised to me for not liking the goat. April apologised to Anne for starting it all off. I apologised to Anne for getting in a mood over it. Michael apologised to me for his mistake. Trev was at the point of setting up a confessional in the hall by the time we'd all finished. I must say being sorry and forgiving others gets easier with practice. Just had a thought: God must spend all day every day forgiving people. Wonder if he ever gets tired of people saying sorry for the same things over and over again. Wonder if he gets tired of *me* saying sorry for the same things over and over again. This is a very troubling personal thought.

Had one very good thought at bed-time: if I hadn't made the mistake then I wouldn't have met Val, the goat lady, who wouldn't in turn have come to the turkey-boning, wouldn't have heard of Jesus and definitely wouldn't have come to our church. Lord, you work in mysterious ways. Why do I have to have a goat as my cross?

Thursday 26th December

Loads of friends round today for a walk in the afternoon, a mega left-overs meal and mad games of 'Pictionary' and 'Call my bluff' in the evening. All the 'nowhere to go at Christmas' folk came: Christian, pagan and 'definitely interested'. Felt a warm glow at being part of such a big group of happy folk. The pagan neighbours are always surprised that the church members are quite sane and normal; they don't realise how carefully chosen they are. Do wish the Christians wouldn't cheat at the games.

Friday 27th December

Post-Christmas recovery day. Sleep and plenty of Andrew's liver salts.

Saturday 28th December

Alice and Tim having some friends round tonight. They would like food provided and then the rest of the family to disappear. They suggested we might not want to return until 1 am. Strange how teenage offspring are unwilling to trust their parents; I thought it was meant to be the other way round.

Trev gave the 'We are really trusting you to be responsible' talk and I did the 'We will be very disappointed if you let us down' bit, with the 'no alcohol' warning thrown in. Deposited Michael and Susannah with friends for the night and retreated to Mitzi and David's house to sit it out. Worried about them the entire evening, especially about gate-crashers and alcohol and drugs and potential disturbance of the neighbours. Trev stopped me phoning home and pretending it was a wrong number so I could assess the noise level etc. He called it paranoid; I called it reasonable parental concern. Why do cares have the habit of wriggling back into my brain after I've cast them on the Lord? They're like hyperactive homing pigeons. Eventually gave up on trust. Sneaked out Mitzi's back door into the car and cruised past our house with Mitzi in tow, at about 11.30 pm. All the lights in the house on and loud music pounding out onto the street. Mitzi hopped out of the car, scurried round the back and had a look inside. She had to beat a fairly hasty retreat when Tim spotted her and came out the back door in pursuit. Raced off at top speed lest he see our car retreating into the distance. Most nerve-wracking moment. It is very, very hard to let go and trust teenagers. You imagine it like the TV ads say – moustaches on the paintings and scratches on the furniture, at the very least.

Why is their whole world different from mine? They don't even start at the same safe starting points, like the previously assumed-for-Christians no sex before marriage. You have to bang it into their heads with the subtlety of a JCB digger, pretending all the time that you understand them. I've about as much hope of understanding them as I have of convincing John Wimber that spiritual gifts are not for today. Why can't they have a built-in Christian homing device?

Left Mitzi and David's in good time but stopped by the river on the way home, just to talk for a moment or two. It was lovely to have some peace and quiet. When we got in, Tim and Alice were not pleased. Alice said, 'We were really worried about you. Where were you? We expected you home at 1 am and it's after 2 o'clock now. It was too late for us to phone Mitzi and David's. Where have you been?' Had to confess to not having noticed the time passing. A subtle role reversal seems to be setting into this relationship. Surely *I'm* meant to worry about *them?* God, help me to understand teenagers.

Still, it's very nice to be loved enough to be worried about.

Sunday 29th December

Invited out for lunch today at the Priddles. This is always a culinary extravaganza. Though the benefits of a Priddle lunch always need to be balanced against the dangers of a Priddle assault, on home territory. There's really no escape when you've just been served an Egon Ronay look-alike; you can't just excuse yourself and hurry home. Today we had pear and stilton, roast rib of beef with all the trimmings and chocolate truffle torte. (Even Alice and Tim are prepared to make the sacrifice of an afternoon with middle-aged church members to eat this well.) This makes me feel inadequate and mildly jealous, and Trev feel sleepy – there's nothing like a good ten-pointer, enthusiastically preached, followed by an excellent lunch, to make the preacher lapse into an exhausted stupor. Never know why he doesn't sympathise with the congregation when they momentarily close their eyes *during* a ten-pointer. Sermon indigestion seems to be quite a common experience.

Should have been ready for the formation attack when it came. Usual warning signs – Pris out in front with an apparently innocent comment, 'You know I've been wondering about how we organise the supply preaching in church,' Sam flanking with, 'I was wondering about that too. In fact, I think the choice of preachers when you're away needs to be seriously reconsidered.' Followed by Pris homing into the main reason for the lunch invitation. 'I think Sam would be wonderful at preaching, and I know how highly you think of him, Pastor. You'd have him promoted from deacon to elder tomorrow if you had your way, wouldn't you?' Trev seriously out-manoeuvered at this stage, and rousing himself to the full heights of his ministerial training in damage control and people management (usually general, bumbling affirmation, just a hint of exaggeration, a little tact, a measure of ambiguity and deferring the decision to a later date).

'Yes, yes of course. Sam's just the kind of man we need in leadership.' (Very significant exaggeration this time.)

'I know his message for the children last year was widely commented on. It was quite remarkable how he managed to rewrite the whole of Romans in rap.' (Masterly use of ambiguity; it produced eight phone calls of complaint and two letters. More than any single sermon of Trev's has ever registered. Thank goodness.)

'Though we'll have to take time to consider it fully, look at it from every angle.' (Excellent postponing shot.)

'We know how very hard you work, Pastor, in fact we're concerned about your health. Sam would be happy to share your load. He's always a willing worker.' (Shock tactics: sympathy for the Pastor *and* appreciation of his industry. Trev constitutionally unable to reply to this very rare approach. Wifely intervention needed.)

'It's great when people of discernment like your-selves appreciate Trev's hard work. Preaching's so evidently his gift.' (Flattery; clear, grovelling desire for another Priddle lunch, and appeal to the biblical principle of gifting.)

'Oh, Sam could never hope to emulate Trev. But he's learned *so* much from Trev's approach to Scripture.' (Overwhelming flattery tactics. Trev's resistance wilting. Wife's quick thinking needed.)

'You know, I thought Sam's real gift was in organ-ising, getting things done, administration. That kind of thing. The way he organised the autumn outreach couldn't have been bettered.' (Turn the conversation in a different direction. Speak the truth – ever so slightly overstated.)

'And as for you Pris, we all know about your gift of hospitality – your cooking is legendary, and your desire to witness. You make such a good team; your gifts complement each other.' (Slight twisting of the biblical gift of hospitality there.)

'Well, I'd like Sam to do something up front. Get the recognition he deserves.' (Moment of honesty. Dangerous feeling of sympathy for Pris's wifely concern. Could lead to unwise comment. Over to Trev.)

'I really understand, but at the end of the day, Pris, we do what we do for an audience of one. Though maybe we need to speak our appreciation of each other more openly. We all need encouragement and I'm so touched by your concern for me.' (Sensed the danger of Sam ever reaching the pulpit easing.)

'I believe God has blessed you with strong, definite gifts, Sam, but I'm not sure they're to be in the pulpit. I see the gift of administration in you and there's compassion too. I'd work more on those. How would you feel about organising a men's ministry, for instance? Spearhead the organisational side, get it up and running?'

You could see Sam glow with praise and the excitement of something to get working on.

'We'll get together soon and talk it over more fully.'
Game, set and match, God!

Monday 30th December

Phone call from Sam first thing this morning with a list of people he has contacted since yesterday and a full run-down of potential speakers for the new men's meeting. He suggested himself as the opening speaker for mid-January with Gordon McDonald and Floyd McClung to follow. When Trev mentioned that they might not be available at such short notice he said he was willing to give them his opening slot as an alternative. Is this the gift of faith? Or presumption?

The small matter of finance does not seem to be a problem for Sam. He feels that it is the Lord's job to look after those in his employment and he imagines that such well-known people will have more than enough funds to pay their own way, and the usual £5 book token should be a sufficient honorarium. Trev left open-mouthed.

Tuesday 31st December

Joint churches' watch-night service. Content: a carefully blended mixture of the non-offensive to Christians of any persuasion whatsoever. Venue: this year the Anglican church, the choice being based on an even more carefully worked-out rota, clearly seen to be a fair balance in relation to numbers in membership of each church and including all the Christian meeting places in our area. (Except, of course, those who refuse to meet together with other Christians at all since they would be contaminated by association.) Wonder how they'll manage in heaven. Will they have a separate area there too? A legal document outlining terms and conditions may have to be drawn up and the possibility of involving The United Nations in the pre-service negotiations are being considered for next year. I think we may have misunderstood the notion of the church militant.

Switched off from church politics and just enjoyed it. Forgot I wasn't meant to because it was in a 'bastion of liberalism' according to Sybil Sharpe. I think I could happily be an Anglican. There's a certain comfort in the sense of order and pattern. I love the hushed atmosphere, the stained-glass windows and the full sound of a pipe organ. Felt all tingly and really sensed God there. Sybil Sharpe says God likes things to be plain. All I can say is, he must have changed his mind since creation then.

Wednesday 1st January

Trev is investigating the possibility of us going on a retreat week with a 'time for meditation and the daily Eucharist'. I am not sure I can handle a Eucharist, especially one a day. Why can't they call it 'The Lord's Table' or 'Communion' like we do? There are bound to be candles and people in robes swinging incense and that funny high-pitched kind of singing. Have decided I am not going to go. Maybe I couldn't be an Anglican after all.

Told Trev that I do not feel led to go. Trev looked at me knowingly and said there was no such phrase as 'feel led' in Scripture. I said I would make it a matter for prayer. Hope he doesn't know how I'm really feeling. I am not feeling threatened.

Thursday 2nd January

Annual clandestine swap of congregational Christmas gifts between the rectory and the manse. Clearly our congregation thinks we are in serious need of sustenance, especially in the form of chocolate biscuits. Is this better than the rectory, where they're inundated by soap, last year's unwanted bath salts, and various other sundry smelly items? Are non-conformist ministers supposed to be hungry and Anglican ministers dirty? Maybe somebody will do a theological thesis some time on the distribution of gifts according to denomination.

Loaded up the car under cover of darkness with Michael and Susannah doing look-out in case any member of the congregation should appear. When we arrived, Gwen and Rob had their piles of unwanted shower gel, banana hair mousse, bath scrub grains and grapefruit soap at the ready. We had a good selection of chocolates, creams and plains. Totally amicable exchange. We ignore the value of each gift and just do a straight swap, gift for gift. It usually works out fairly well; in the end they balance each other out. It's surprising how different gifts can be handled totally harmoniously. Why can't spiritual gifts be as easily dealt with?

It's also surprising how two such different ministers get on so well together. This augurs well for heaven. Had a reassuring thought; since we will not be having communion in heaven (at least not like now), we won't have to have a name for it. Wanted to ask what Gwen and Rob call 'communion' in their church but didn't dare since Trev would realise why. Maybe I should go to one of their communion services soon so I can prove to Trev that that's not the problem – even though it is.

Discovered that the Pentecostal pastor mostly gets pot plants. Wonder why? Does this mean he's into growth? Maybe we could arrange a three-way swap with him next year.

Friday 3rd January

Phoned Gwen to ask her about communion within the Anglican communion, so to speak. Theirs is actually called 'Holy Communion', though I don't think it can be any more holy than ours. All my worst fears confirmed; apparently Eucharists are high church with candles, incense and the works. Gwen was amazed that I didn't know such obvious things. Felt like some lowly off-shoot of a minor branch of a breakaway twig of a sect. Also felt significantly unspiritual and of lesser holiness, and had to pretend I was just checking up on the finer details for Alice's non-existent, A-level Religious Knowledge essay on 'Forms of worship in another denomination'.

Saturday 4th January

Rob called with a folder on Anglicanism for Alice; unfortunately Trev was in and took delivery. Wanted to run away at tea-time. Winked frantically and pathetically at Alice when Trev gave her the folder. The problem with this is that my left eye doesn't know what the right one is doing and refuses to operate independently, so I have a sort of double-eye wink which I supplement with a nodding action for purposes of reinforcement. My futile attempts at winking look like a sort of preliminary bow before a Sumo wrestling match or a failed but repeated attempt to reach a 'bowed in prayer' position. Alice did not co-operate, 'Is something wrong with your eyes, Mum?' Had to tell Trev the folder was really for me and that Gwen must have got confused. Then had to declare an interest in Anglicanism. Trev floored me when he said, 'I believe it's the Eucharist that interests you actually, dear.' How does he know me so well? At least he spared me from total embarrassment in front of Alice.

I *will* go to the meditation and Eucharist week. If Gwen can handle a Eucharist then so can I.

Sunday 5th January

Val, the goat lady, back in church again. She asked me how Billy was doing. Couldn't quite bring myself to say, 'Very smelly, thank you.' I will have to buy him some perfume – or maybe that should be after-shave.

Caught Trev at the end of the morning hand-shake conga, in the act of inviting the Priddles round for a meal. Dementia must be setting in. He is fully aware that I become a totally unco-ordinated, panic-stricken, nightmare-ridden, quivering wreck at the very thought of cooking for Pris Priddle. It's like having Delia Smith round for tea. Did my best to avoid catastrophe: manufactured several evening speaking engagements, a committee meeting, an evening class and even a Tupperware party. Realised that this was merely putting off the evil day. They are coming on Friday 17th.

Lunch was not a pleasant affair. I did not need to be told that the gift of hospitality has little to do with cooking. Nor do I think it is a gift given only to women. If we are earnestly to desire spiritual gifts then Trev had better have hands laid on him for the gift of hospitality, definitely not my hands and preferably before Friday week. Told Trev that if he was so keen to have the Priddles round then he could jolly well help, and that he may as well start learning how to cook now. Was not impressed when he asked how to mash potatoes and poured all the meat juices for the gravy down the sink. Discovered that two in the kitchen make considerably more mess than one. Holiness at home is very hard.

Monday 6th January

Came home to find Egon Hansford making the evening meal, two tins of freshly-opened baked beans nestling beneath a generous helping of prime, mushed-up corned beef and the whole smothered in a sumptuous, if slightly gritty, layer of Smash instant potato. Kind of Cordon Orange, Puce and Off-white. It is a start. Though I'm not sure if Pris could find words adequate to describe it. I think she might have to depend very fully on the Lord to make her truly thankful.

Tuesday 7th January

Trev too busy to have a day off yesterday – no doubt planning his evening culinary masterpiece. Tried to get him to arrange time together later this week but he says he is far too busy and he needs to leave time for pastoral counselling and visitation. Will have to work something out. Had a good idea. Told Trev that someone wanted to see him urgently and that I'd suggested this Friday evening at 8 pm. Watched him pencil it into the counselling slot in his diary. Nearly thrown when he asked who it was, but just said they hadn't mentioned their name.

Wednesday 8th January

Trev asked who I thought wanted to see him on Friday and if I recognised the voice. He just assumes someone phoned. Said I'd never heard that voice before on the phone.

Thursday 9th January

Mitzi called to ask me to go to the cinema with her tomorrow. I do so want to see 'The Crucible'. Thought of telling Trev that the mystery caller had cancelled, and going out with Mitzi instead. After all a husband cannot fulfil all one's needs. Held fast and said I had a prior arrangement. Can't wait till tomorrow evening.

Friday 10th January

Really excited about tonight; a whole uninterrupted evening with Trev. We can sit in his study and have time for the kind of in-depth chat he has with counsellees. First he will put me at my ease with general conversation, then we will have a relaxing cup of coffee, then he will encourage me to share how I feel.

Trev is quite edgy about who is coming this evening. Think he wonders if it is a criticiser or one of those difficult spaghetti, pastoral situations that requires serious unscrambling.

Got changed and put some make-up on after tea, then went out the back door, round to the front of the house and rang the door bell. Took a while for Trev to catch on. He wondered what I was doing there. I said that I had an appointment to see the Rev and there were some things I wanted to talk over. Trev gasped, 'You, you . . . you're the mystery caller! You let me get worked up and worried and concerned and all the time it was you!' Things did not work out quite as planned. Trev was so stunned that he retreated to the study, muttering about the incomprehensibility of women.

Cried. Then phoned Mitzi and went to see 'The Crucible'. Didn't enjoy it at all, just sat struggling with who Trev belongs to, me or the church. I don't mind sharing him but I'd like some of what's left over when everybody else has had their bit. Felt selfish and guilty, then felt justified and indignant, then felt selfish and guilty all over again. Think the answer is

that Trev belongs to God. Wish the congregation realised this too.

Mitzi tried to help. She thinks we need a little more
romance in our lives. I am not to demand time, I am to
be subtle and seductive. Surely seductive is bad, like
Delilah?

Trev repentant and full of apologies on my return.
We are to have significant time together on Monday.

Saturday 11th January

Mitzi called to offer some practical help. She suggested a bottle of wine and some grapes at bed-time.
Normally Trev and I have hot chocolate and maltesers. She also thought a change from the cosy tartan
pyjamas would be a good idea and she had a little gift
for me. It was little. It's so good to receive such practical pastoral help from a member of the congregation.
Wish she had brought a hot-water bottle too.

Trev and I had a wonderful evening together.

Sunday 12th January

Mitzi has suggested a proper pastoral care team just
for us. She spoke to our elder, Ned, at the morning
service today. He told her that he *had* given us biscuits
already, and some maltesers, but anything she wanted
him to do, he would try the best he could. Mitzi has an
amazing gift of getting her own way. I think it may
have something to do with how she uses her eye-

lashes. She does wear as much make-up as gravity will allow.

We are to be officially loved and cared for. Can't wait.

Monday 13th January

Official day off. Trev very positive. Talked about developing a creative hobby together instead of endlessly talking about the church. Sometimes life in the manse feels like a rerun of 'Ever-decreasing Circles'. Ministry needs a little perspective and variety to be effective. Considered various possibilities. Trev feels fly-fishing is a potential winner. I'm more inclined to free-fall parachuting. They say opposites attract. Clearly we need to find some middle ground. Discussed walking (too wet), golf (too ministerially predictable), cycling (only one bike), gardening (killer fingers), fitness suite (too embarrassingly flabby), swimming (can't).

Inspiration struck tonight. Saw a wonderful vicar on TV who is into wild and wacky interior design. We will redecorate the house in a creative and individual way. Apparently this is possible on a limited budget if one uses special paint effects and home carpentry. This vicar's congregation didn't seem to mind what could only be described as a highly original approach. His living-room ceiling was painted in rays of dark blue and yellow, with stars on the blue bit, and the walls were pillar-box red. I am all for originality.

Got a bit carried away in 'Paint Craft'. I plan to

stencil, colour-wash, marble, rag-roll and distress (wood that is). I will buy a book on carpentry tomorrow. Trev thinks I am moving too fast and that the whole scheme needs deliberation, planning and looking at from every angle, and we would be best to wait till the finances are in hand. Sounded like he'd swallowed a committee. Where did spontaneity and enthusiasm go to? I want to move out in boldness in at least one area of my life, preferably before my eightieth birthday. I am tired of walking through church treacle.

Tuesday 14th January

Priddle supper approaching. I am very experienced at 'Chicken à la condensed mushroom soup' and 'Jelly with tinned mandarin oranges' but they don't seem quite right. Wish there was a basic 'Cooking for the Congregation' course offered at Bible colleges, for all those who have previously lived on toast. Though it has to be said there is a lot you can do with toast.

Searched through the cookery books. Then prayed before sticking a pin in the index. Came up with 'Chicken with sherry vinegar and tarragon sauce'. Sounds impressive. Had to stick the pin in three more times before it came up with a dessert (could have ended up with home-made pesto sauce or American blue-cheese dressing for afters). Wonder if I can be sure this is the Lord's leading. Maybe I should have used the 'throw the cookery book up in the air and see where it opens' method instead.

Wednesday 15th January

Was asked to conduct a funeral today. Simon, the little boy from next door, arrived with a deceased mouse named Maurice. He was most disappointed when I told him Trev was out, since he wanted his mouse to have a proper funeral, done by a proper minister. We discussed the possibilities over a glass of coke, while the rodent's remains rested on the back-door step. Relieved to discover that he was not in favour of mouse cremation, though the advanced state of decay of the mouse suggested fairly immediate action. Since he had encountered a real funeral before, he was fully aware of the necessities. We discussed flowers, coffin, prayers and burial plot. Helped him arrange an old shoe box and some fake Christmas poinsettias and chose a spot in our rockery since his mother wanted nothing to do with the beast. Trev still not home. Why is he never here when he is needed? He's home about as much as a lifer doing time in Broadmoor!

Two more cokes and three chocolate biscuits later, Trev still not home on parole. Maurice showing signs of squirming, inner life.

Felt more than a little uncomfortable putting on a dog collar, but apparently this is 'very important' for all funerals. Simon clearly disappointed. He wanted a 'white nightie over the top' for it to be a 'proper funeral'. Tried to explain that I didn't have a surplice, then remembered that I did have an appropriately coloured nightie. Made the ultimate sacrifice. Saying mouse prayers in the open air in your nightie and a dog collar is not a comfortable experience.

Should have known that Trev, Michael and Susannah would make their entrance just after I had commenced mouse prayers. Was forced to continue as if nothing had happened while they watched. Gritted my teeth and warned them into silence with a look that would have killed. I am supposed to have said, 'We thank you, Lord, that this mouse was a good mouse, a mouse much loved by all his friends. He was a mouse who lived well and who ran his wheel with joy. Thank you that Simon will meet his beloved mouse, Maurice, in heaven one day. In Jesus' name, Amen.' But I am sure this was greatly exaggerated. They all sobered up considerably when I asked Michael and Susannah to be the pallbearers and Trev to do the committal.

Knew there would be Anglican nightie jokes all through tea-time. Was not disappointed. Had to listen to 'That nightie was definitely "surplus" to requirements' and 'You mitre waited till Dad got home, Mum.'

Hope Simon was happy with it all.

Thursday 16th January

Old Mrs Leith whose house backs onto ours tells me she saw 'yesterday's goings on' in the garden. Saw my white robe quite clearly through her binoculars. Says she 'don't want none o' that white magic stuff round here'. Tried to explain that I was only burying a mouse. If I'd said I'd been speaking incantations over a disembowelled frog she couldn't have been any more appalled. Tempted just to give up and do

'Double, double toil and trouble. Fire burn and cauldron bubble' in my old crone voice. Why do I feel like doing totally shocking and rebellious things sometimes? Maybe it's my age.

Stuck it out and eventually managed to register the truth. She looked at me with a mixture of disbelief and pity. Then went off muttering, 'And her a Rev's wife too!'

Mavis Gladhope phoned about 'God doing a new thing'. I said I was very pleased.

Ned, our senior elder, phoned about 'needing a period of stability in the church and not bringing in anything new at the moment'. Agreed with him too. Think he must have heard about the Priddle initiative in men's ministries, though he didn't actually say so. There is a definite skill in decoding church members' comments. Maybe he's feeling threatened.

Sybil Sharpe phoned to protest about 'the invasion of new songs' in church recently. Murmured sympathetically, though didn't actually say anything. Maybe I'm getting better at tact.

Louise Bell phoned to say how much she's enjoying the worship these days.

Think Trev should put them all on a committee together.

Friday 17th January

Had no time to go over the Priddle supper recipes due to unforeseen mouse burying and surfeit of congregational calls. Asked God for special culinary help, though cannot see any biblical precedence for this. Manna is not exactly what I have in mind, can't remember what Elijah was fed but I'm sure it didn't require a recipe book, and Martha didn't get a lot of encouragement for her culinary efforts. Come to think about it, spices and garlic were what the Israelites had to leave behind, and all Adam and Eve ate presumably was fruit and veg. Remembered that God likes the aroma of roast meat. This is more promising though I must say it had always struck me as slightly odd. On this basis maybe all I should serve is bread, fruit and meat.

Doesn't seem quite right to leave 'Chicken in sherry vinegar' and 'Mint mousse' in God's hands. Left them there anyway since they're better there than in mine.

Started with the mousse. The first two attempts produced a runny, stringy, granular mass. Eventually had to add a double portion of gelatine to make it set. Still, God's into double portions too. By this stage I had used rather a lot of 'After Eights' which, according to the recipe, were to be 'sandwiched between the layers of mousse and cut into diagonals to decorate the top'. Had to keep running to and fro to the corner shop for more, getting more and more exhausted. Must have covered at least three miles. Very embarrassing, so tried to explain about the mousse. From the strange looks I got this may have made it worse. On the third trip the shop assistant asked me if mints were part of the mouse-burying ritual and how was the white goat involved? She whispered that she would quite like a mystical experience too. Mrs Leith's neighbourhood grape-vine is clearly effective. Had no time to explain.

Dread my next visit. I think I may have sullied my Christian witness in the neighbourhood.

Hoped the chicken would be more straightforward. It was. Golden-brown chicken and shallots looked great. Cheated and bought some ready mixed, fancy salad leaves – begrudged the £1.79 on rabbit food.

7.30 pm. Relief; all is well.

Wore my special evening wear. Felt great. Noticed Sam looking at me the way I've seen him looking at Mitzi.

Just as well I tasted the chicken sauce before I served it. Overwhelming taste of vinegar. Not quite sure what I did wrong; maybe I confused the 150 mls of sherry vinegar with the 450 mls of sherry. It did look like a lot of vinegar, but then you can always trust Delia implicitly. Clearly though, you can't trust an imbecile who can't even read Delia. Panic; all the remaining sherry now inside various people, none left to add to the offending sauce to redress the balance. Thought about what I could substitute to swamp the chip-shop flavour. Surveyed the larder. Very tempted by the familiar rows of condensed mushroom soup but tried to think creatively and step out into uncharted vinegar in faith. Copious quantities of orange juice seemed like a possible solution, but none in the house. Did some rapid deep breathing and tried to remain calm. Sent Tim on an errand of mercy for orange juice to the corner shop, with instructions to go out through the Priddle-infested dining area non-chalantly, pretending the money he had to ask Trev for en route was for milk, then run like the clappers to the shop, purchase the orange juice and some milk (so it would look like I genuinely needed milk), pass the orange-juice carton in through the kitchen window rather than walking past the Priddles, then come in the front door bearing the aforementioned milk and walk casually into the kitchen with it. Was forced to pay one pound in bribery money for all of this.

Just after Tim left I had an excellent creative Christian thought – PRAYER. 'Lord, just as you turned the water into wine please could you turn *vinegar* into wine right now. This should be even easier since it's sherry vinegar, so presumably there won't be so much changing to do – and I don't need even one jar full, just 450 mls would do, though you don't have to be exact. Since you did the first miracle to save embarrassment you must understand how I feel. Please do it now Lord. Amen.'

Tasted the sauce in faith. Evidently not enough faith. Still vinegary. Realised I had forgotten the 'In Jesus' name' at the end of the prayer. Wasn't sure whether this was obligatory in panic situations. I'm sure God doesn't refuse on a mere technicality, at least I hope not. Prayed again, most earnestly, walking round the kitchen and raising my hands in the air, 'Please Lord, save this chicken, in Jesus' name. Amen.' Sudden awareness of what I'd just prayed. Increasing panic must've produced total irrationality. 'Lord, I'd like to correct that, please. It's not actual *salvation* for the chicken I want. I know you don't save chickens, and anyway this one's been dead and frozen for a little while already and so it would have been too late for him to find his way to you, even if you did want some chickens in heaven, which I sincerely hope you don't.

Please just forget the chicken and save the sauce. And my reputation. In Jesus' name. Amen.'

Thankfully, Tim appeared just then at the kitchen window with the orange juice. A carton of orange juice and a dose of cornflour later and all seemed well. Relief. It did taste like 'Chicken in orange juice' rather than 'Chicken in sherry vinegar' though. Adrenalin flow ceased and exhaustion began to set in.

Had a horrible thought as I was serving it up. What if God had answered my prayer to turn the vinegar into wine *after* I'd added the orange juice, maybe as I'd carried it to the table? One of those eleventh-hour answers to prayer after you've all but given up. Maybe God was just testing my faith all the time, so I'd learn to trust him and not depend on my own resources. If he turned the vinegar to wine now, the whole thing would taste awful. Begged God silently that he would ignore all the prayers I'd prayed about the vinegar and not answer them at all, and that if he had answered them that he would undo whatever he had done and just leave everything as it had been when I'd left the kitchen. Told him I'd try to sort out my scrambled praying later, if that was OK with him. Chicken tasted remarkably good. Breathed a 'Thank you, Lord, for not answering my first prayer and for answering my last prayer. I think it's best, all things considered, that you remain in control, rather than me.'

Bit of a guilty feeling when Pris asked for the recipe. Reckon she was only testing to see if I'd cheated and bought the whole lot in the chill cabinet of some supermarket. Replied quite casually that it was just one of my personal variations on a Delia recipe and that God sometimes gave me creative inspiration in the kitchen – could have added, 'Especially in the area of prayer and condensed soup, in fact there isn't anything I can't do with condensed soup.'

Pride dealt a mega blow with the mousse. Saw Pris engage in digging and sawing actions with her spoon. The mousse resisted like a trampoline, a lot of give but no breakthrough. Pris said, 'What a most interesting texture, dear! A sort of firm jelly with a bouncy feel. One ought to watch one's eyes really as the spoon ricochets on its upward trajectory. A lovely flavour though.' I fume when I am called 'dear'. Unless the speaker is at least seventy and has kind eyes, it is patronising while pretending to be pleasant. I am not Pris Priddle's 'dear'. In fact I am not anyone's 'dear' at all. I am an abject failure at cooking and most other domestic tasks. I am incapable of even basic hospitality. Why Lord, if you could feed 5,000, couldn't you have helped me feed four successfully? Why couldn't you have given me the gift of hospitality that 1 Timothy says I have to have to be a proper pastor's wife? And why did you make that gift obligatory? It isn't fair.

Went to bed feeling very sorry for myself.

Saturday 18th January

Val, the goat lady, called. Didn't even attempt proper manse entertainment in the front room with the little coffee tables, the china cups and the obligatory napkins; there's no point. Sat her down in the kitchen with a mug of instant coffee and a digestive biscuit straight from the tin. Didn't try to evangelise her either. I'm fed up trying to do the right things and getting them in a horrible muddle, when you can't even bury a mouse or make a mousse, or get a Christmas present for your own sister right, come to that, then you feel like giving up. I would like to be allowed to be a perfectly normal, permitted-to-fail individual. I would like to have an ordinary non-Christian friend without being obliged to produce instant transformation and feeling guilty if I don't introduce the four spiritual laws, explain them page by page, issue a personal challenge at the end and produce a gloriously saved triumph of grace to the church the next Sunday. Didn't even try to wangle the conversation; chatted about this and that as if I *was* normal, whatever that is. I do want her to become a Christian but I don't want to drive her into it. It should be like falling in love, not like an arranged marriage. Told her what a failure I felt as a Christian, how hard it was sometimes and how even harder it was to be a ministry wife. Strange, this didn't feel like letting God down, just liberatingly honest. Wish you could be as honest with Christians and still be accepted.

Sunday 19th January

Sat with Val in church. Didn't even consider spiritual brownie points rating. Didn't care if anybody saw or not.

Sam Priddle went to the front to announce the commencement of Men's Ministries. Sam has a special 'spiritual' voice for such occasions; very loud and rising in pitch until you think he can't possibly go any higher, then he suddenly drops down on the last word of each sentence like a meteorite plummeting to earth. His face gets redder and redder, his eyes bulge and he always grips both sides of the lectern. Gradually his hands creep further and further forward until his whole upper body is hovering over the edge. Every eye is so totally focused on the precarious tilt of the lectern that nobody listens to a word he's saying. While this is happening the entire congregation instinctively start to lean forward in their seats too, in anticipation of a potential crash. The whole procedure is so reminiscent of an elaborate mating ritual that you can imagine a hushed, David Attenborough voice-over: 'Now the male is in full display; the gradual forward movement, the rising call, the gripping hand movements are all power signals. He transfixes the younger males with special threatening eye movements. This is a territorial marking ritual which indicates leadership in the territory over which his call can be heard. It is a warning to other males to retreat.' How true.

The more nervous Sam gets the more he engages in verbal spraying. This is particularly unpleasant if you are in the front row, who are forced to use their hymn books as protection against random sprinkling. This morning was a torrential downpour.

'Men's ministries will commence on the second Tuesday of each successive month, with the exception of this January, and save for the summer season, when we will have a short rest from spiritual sustenance for the male of the species.' (Toothy smile followed by a 'Haw, haw, haw'.) 'Our first subject is "Symbols of success in secular society", and the speaker is Cecil Sanderson.'

This level of sprinkling is totally unacceptable in a Baptist church.

At the end of the service, Pris reminded us of how powerful Sam was in public speaking. 'I looked round,' she said, 'and clearly no one could take their eyes off him. He holds an audience spellbound.' Personally, I think they're more spit-bound.

First official meeting of the pastoral care team today. It is to be chaired by Ned our elder, with Earnest to give spiritual counsel, Mitzi's husband, Dave, providing the youthful balance (he is, after all, only forty-two) and Mavis Gladhope as the token woman.

They *prayed* for us! *They* prayed for us! They prayed for *us*! They prayed *for* us! Nearly cried. This is the first ever church meeting where we have been totally on the receiving end. Felt almost guilty. I don't think I know *how* to receive; it doesn't feel quite right. We are to meet them again on Thursday to share our needs.

Monday 20th January

Started on the manse decoration today. My main aim is to un-beige our home; if God used such a riot of

97

colour in creation then the manse should reflect his colour choices too. I am determined not to do things in half-measures. Bought some sunshine yellow paint to sponge Michael's bedroom and hide the plaster patches where bits of paint have peeled off along with his posters. Sponging is harder than we thought. By mid-morning it looked as if a serial egg scrambler had run amok in a hen house and flung dozens of freshly laid eggs at the wall. I think it will take a while for Trev and I to grasp the subtlety of sponging. We may have to cover the first blobby egg-yolk efforts with football posters, but the second half was a masterpiece of understatement, if only due to running out of paint and having to water it down towards the end. I think we have developed a new decorating technique – the graduated look. Bright colour gradually fading to a much paler colour; egg-yolk yellow easing into palest primrose. Maybe we should invite *Houses and Gardens* to come and do a photo feature on the Hansford hen-house effect. I think we have another area of obvious gifting here.

Since our bedroom looks as if it fell out of a second-hand shop, which is not surprising since it did, we thought we'd go for what the interior design programme called 'a unifying theme' to 'bring together interestingly diverse objects of individual interest'. The idea was to buy lengths of cheap muslin, dip them in a plaster-of-paris mixture, drape them over our tatty wardrobe, then swirl them in classical curves rapidly before they dried. This looked very good on the TV interior design show. On our wardrobe it looked like lengths of cheap muslin swathed in cement, hanging dolefully in limp, pale grey goo. When it had dried we made the nasty discovery that the wardrobe doors would no longer close. Decided to leave the bedroom with its 'unique piece' as a 'focal point', rather than attempt the classical marbling we had planned for the walls. Why do books describe as 'a two-hour transformation' what would have taken Michael Angelo weeks? My personal, spiritual transformation works at about the same speed. Encouraged by that thought; maybe I'll be a spiritual masterpiece someday. Trev caught me at coffee-time muttering to God, 'Lord, make me like the Sistine chapel ceiling for you.' Sybil Sharpe would've been particularly horrified.

Next job was to distress the lounge coffee tables. Since they have already been distressed by a wide variety of congregational coffee mugs making circular, white patterns, further intentional distressing could not do much harm. Trev could not understand the point of deliberately making something look older than it actually is. When I told him it was the 'in' thing, and that I didn't particularly like it either but that we needed to upgrade our boring traditional image, he gave up.

He was quite relieved when Earnest, as part of the pastoral care team, arrived round with a going cheap, job lot of beige and off-white wallpaper sent to us by Derek and Sybil Sharpe as a 'love gift'. I have painted it lime green as an act of protest.

The house is definitely beginning to take on an individual air.

Tuesday 21st January

Val called round for coffee. She says she likes the distressed tables. They make her feel comfortable. I think Val is becoming a real live friend.

Wesley Tweed called round to sit on the sofa. I am not sure why. He is still putting things in the Lord's hands, but I don't quite know what.

Wednesday 22nd January

Mid-week prayer meeting tonight. Nearly didn't go but was glad I did in the end. Real sense of God's presence – initially anyway. How is it that I can find the right words to pray when I'm with others and God seems real and almost tangible, but when I'm alone all I can think about is how I can concoct the evening meal out of fridge scraps and whether I'll have time to get to the post office before it closes?

Old Albert brought the mid-week prayer meeting to a spectacular halt this evening. We were all most earnestly praying for renewal and revival and showers of blessing and God moving in the nation and breaking Satan's strongholds. We all thought the Spirit was going to come in power, when Albert started singing:

Turn your eyes upon Jesus,
Look full in his wonderful face,
And the things of earth will grow strangely dim
By the light of the silvery moon.

There was a strange, suppressed choking sound from Dave followed by a gathering roar of muffled snorts.

It's a pity Wesley added, 'Yes, Lord, do it by the light of the moon. Amen, Lord. We know you can do it at night-time too, Lord.'

The prayer meeting dissolved in uproar, and Trev had to bring it to an abrupt end. People were bent double, tears streaming down their faces, some were convulsed in the aisle, making what sounded like animal noises and stuffing hankies in their mouths. It did look suspiciously like Toronto. Old Albert couldn't understand why people were drying their eyes. Think he thought the Spirit had come and he'd missed something. Just goes to show, it's difficult to tell the counterfeit from the real.

Thursday 23rd January

Pastoral care team visit. Ned suggested a manse inspection, so had to spend the whole day in rigorous dusting and clearing out unmentionable objects, in a state of terminal decomposition, from under the children's beds. I'm sure Mavis Gladhope would have found a spiritual lesson in this. Used a full bottle of bleach, a can of polish, an aerosol of fresh air spray and a lot of energy. I can testify now to the efficacy of newsprint in window cleaning. Even went as far as cleaning the oven, should they wish to inspect it. Hope they don't feel the need to open any kitchen cupboards or bathroom cabinets. Almost searched beneath Tim's mattress just in case; you can never be sure with a teenage male, however Christian. The whole process made me feel owned; body, mind and soul as well as house. I know they mean well but it felt like an auction preview or like standing in one of those little skimpy white hospital gowns before an awe-inspiring, three-piece-suited surgeon. It emphasises your weakness and his power.

I was not impressed when Ned offered me the coffee tables he had in his loft, which he said were in better condition than mine. Could see Trev smirk. Felt like a charitable trust.

There was no comment on the egg-yolk blobs or the lime-green walls, just an audible, throttled gasp. I could see them all doing mental gymnastics, calculating how many coats of paint will be needed to cover lime green before the next incumbent takes over.

I was afraid to tell any of them what I really needed. How can I say I want to be me and not a ministerial appendage; real and not always keeping up appearances? I will wait and see if they are genuinely going to care before I reveal the real me.

They want to come round and pray with us regularly, just for our own spiritual up-building. Not sure if I feel pleased or threatened by this. What if they find out on closer acquaintance that I am not as spiritual as they thought? Will have to get down to serious Bible study so I can impress them with a few casually dropped-in, obscure, Old Testament references. I do so want to get closer to God too; maybe that will happen when I study more. Getting the outside right is simpler.

Friday 24th January

Went to the Christian bookshop looking for serious Bible study material. Came home with a most impressive scheme. It requires a wide selection of coloured pencils and has a system of complicated symbols. I have always been impressed by those people who have a lot of markings in their Bibles with underlinings and notes in the margins. Now I will be able to be the same.

Started this evening. It needed the whole of the kitchen table for all the coloured pencils, the chart of symbols and the book. Read through the whole system: green crosses for the cross, yellow triangles for New Testament references to the Old Testament, blue circles for promises, red asterisks for warnings, purple stars for the new life, pink ovals for Jesus' words, orange flames for the Holy Spirit, turquoise arrows for prophecies, black blobs (obviously) for Satan. Since this was the only thing that was obvious, most of my time was spent trying to get to grips with the symbol sequence. This rather defeats the point.

Maybe I'll get better at it. Thought I might try to compose a song to help me remember. Lay in bed and worked out something to go to the tune of 'Land of hope and glory'. Was very pleased with the results:

> New, new life in Jesus,
> You're a purple star,
> Pink oval words of the Saviour,

They will take us far.
Red asterisks for warnings
Keep us safe from ill,
Promises in blue circles
All your words fulfil.
Black, black blobs for evil,
Green the cross on high,
Orange flames for the Spirit,
He will teach us to fly.
Yellow triangles, new to old
Make connections clear,
Turquoise arrows point future
Prophecies are near.

The only real problem is the theological uncertainty as to whether the Holy Spirit will teach us to fly. Thought it should be OK since we will meet the Lord in the air. Sang the song over several times to fix it in my mind. It is very satisfying being a lyric writer. Couldn't wait to sing it to Trev. Noticed all was very quiet in the house. Had a horrible thought that they'd all been raptured and I'd been left behind, though didn't think this was possible. I haven't yet sussed out all the 'pre' and 'post' and 'a' positions of the Lord's coming; it seems enough really that he is coming, so I'm a bit unsure about things like raptures and the like. Surely I wouldn't be the only one left behind? I mean, what about Tim and his mitre jokes? Went quietly to investigate. All five of them just happened to be on the landing outside our bedroom door. I was so relieved to see them. They seemed extremely concerned for my well-being; I suppose I must've looked worried about the rapture and such like. Alice said she thought I looked feverish and went to get me a hot drink and a paracetamol. For some strange reason Tim asked me if I liked Jerusalem. Susannah and Michael grinned inanely and asked me to sing them a song but Trev sent them to bed immediately. They're all behaving very strangely.

Trev said he thought I'd been overdoing it and wondered if the pastoral care/manse inspection team had worried me, or if perhaps something else was on my mind. He gave me a relaxing massage and prayed for me. He's such a kind, caring husband.

Saturday 25th January

Had a quiet day. Trev brought breakfast to me in bed, ran me a bath and put on soothing music. Long may this continue! Sang my symbol song in the bath, banging out the rhythm with a plastic duck on the shampoo bottle. Very satisfying, though I think it needs rounding off with a crescendo at the climax, just like the real thing. Couldn't think of any appropriate words. Will work on it later.

Trev abandoned sermon preparation to help with the ironing! What is wrong with him?

Sunday 26th January

Stayed at home from church today – with Trev's encouragement. Mixture of luxurious self-indulgence and guilt. Struggled with my conscience as to whether I would edify my soul with a taped sermon or read a novel. Knew if I started the novel I would immediately forget about the sermon, but if I started the sermon my mind would drift onto the novel. I must be an all-right Christian since the apostle Paul had the same problem. Decided to subjugate the flesh. Considering the content of the sermon, I'm not sure I succeeded. It was an American ministry tape, all about God's blessing, by Hiram B. Fieldswhite III. Hiram says that the more I give to God the more I'll receive and that the Christian should be into harvesting and reaping and blessing. Apparently that's what 'What a man sows that shall he also reap' means. We are to give to ministries of all sorts, especially to the 'Hiram B. Fieldswhite III Harvestime Mission' and God will give back to us more than we gave. It's kind of like a Christian investment account working on at least a 300% interest rate. (I must have missed those figures in the Bible.) Apparently God only gives to those who give to him. Because of honouring God this way, Hiram and his wife Shannon now have three limos, a ranch in Texas, a villa (with pool) in Florida and a private jet. Hiram must have a lot to give away now. Got out my savings book bank account. I could, at a pinch, invest £23.56 in Hiram's Harvestime Mission, if I'm extra careful with the house-keeping money for a week or two. Just think though, we could be eating sirloin steaks soon. Though if I reinvested the profits received from God and then kept on reinvesting each time we could actually go to visit Hiram in Florida.

Thought it through carefully. Although I would rather like a holiday in Florida, there are a few basic flaws. First, I have never seen this principle operate in Scripture. Wasn't Jesus poor? Secondly, if every Christian in the world gave £1 for instance, where would the anticipated £3 return come from, since everybody would be expecting to receive, having given out? This does not make economic sense. Thirdly, what about all the poor Christians who have nothing to give, don't they ever get anything? Fourthly, where does grace fit in? *Undeserved* favour definitely sounds more like God. Fifthly, the friend who loaned us this tape is in debt. Finally, on this basis if I got rid of Sybil Sharpe I might get three Sybil Sharpe look-alikes back!

Grace is a much better idea. Surely God is like a father, giving out surprise presents just to delight you, not a bank manager working out interest payments? Prayed for grace to handle *one* Sybil Sharpe.

It would have been more edifying reading the novel.

Tim told me the SS had been asking after my whereabouts. She noticed I was missing in action, presumed dead. Said she knew that after my last 'little lapse' one Sunday evening, 15th December according to her records, I would be eager to 'redeem' myself in the eyes of 'those who pay the salary'. Since I must be seriously ill she would not call in case of infection, but would leave the church flowers at the manse gate.

Daren't go to church tonight. She knows she has me cornered.

Monday 27th January

Stayed indoors today. It really was terribly cold. Sybil phoned to say she was praying for my recovery. Put on a very weak, trembly voice. I forgot to thank her for the flowers. Trev had to phone her back, thank her and say that I was mentally impaired because of the illness.

Maybe I am.

Can't get the 'Land of hope and glory' song finished. I have lost my green colouring pencil too, so that's the end of prophecy or promises or something equally important. Still, 1 Corinthians says prophecies will end, so maybe it's all right.

Tuesday 28th January

Perhaps I won't have to go to church next Sunday because of my sickness. I feel like I am on holiday. Realise how tired I am of smiling and saying nice things. I don't want to circulate benevolently, with a fixed grin, sympathising with three bad backs, two problems of guidance, and one lost faith; handling tussles over the flower rota; being understanding and sympathetic with a series of unwilling ladies who refuse to help with the next supper because 'It can't possibly be my turn, *dear*!' and remembering the names of everybody's children, grandchildren and second cousins twice removed. Maybe I won't have to go back ever!

Remembered that I'm not actually sick. I must be in a state of rebellion.

Wednesday 29th January

Went out under cover, wearing a headscarf and Trev's ancient trench coat. Can't find the blue pencil now. This is hopeless!

Thursday 30th January

Had Wesley for tea. Wesley is extremely committed and zealous. I am hoping Tim will notice that this is a good thing to be.

Wesley says he would like a help-meet. Tim told him to help himself to all the meat he wanted but that personally he would rather have a 'babe' or a 'chick'. Where did we go wrong? Wesley says he would like to 'go into full-time Christian work'. He is apparently concerned that his body be a fit temple for the Holy Spirit and so he abstains from white bread.

Noticed him smiling inanely at Alice.

Friday 31st January

Very cold out. Bought another thermal vest. Spotted Wesley purchasing some long johns. Stayed at a discreet distance.

Red pencil gone. That probably means most Christian doctrines are now impossible; can't remember which though. This must be what it feels like to be a liberal theologian; half your doctrines gone and the remainder blunt.

Discovered Michael with all the missing colours, working on his geography project. Maybe I should admit defeat. Surely Bible study should be simpler?

Saturday 1st February

Earnest called to see if he could borrow a sunset. Was a little puzzled at first. I am happy to lend all manner of things but I don't generally keep sunsets handy. Apparently Earnest and Grace are showing their missionary slides tomorrow evening after the service and don't have the obligatory Christian sunset finale slide. Found one or two sunsets but they didn't seem quite right. Aren't you meant to have silhouetted giraffes or a few acacia trees in a barren, sun-dried landscape? Earnest went away happy with 'Sunset over a Scottish loch with pine trees' and 'Sunset over Cornish harbour with fishing boats'. I think his eyesight may be failing and I am not sure the audience are going to be convinced. I'm fairly sure Lake Victoria doesn't have lighthouses and lobster pots.

Sunday 2nd February

Put on Alice's skin lightener, so I would look like I was recovering from severe illness. Tried to look slightly distraught. This was not difficult. It is difficult being honest though, when people ask you if you're feeling better, if you've never been ill in the first place. Tried 'I think I was just a little tired really'. Thanked Sybil profusely for the flowers; one small dust-laden bunch of limp carnations bought from a petrol station forecourt.

African slide show went well. They all noticed the fishing boats and pine trees but nobody minded; in fact Earnest used them to challenge us about what slide show we each could have put on of what we'd been doing at home. He wasn't harsh and judgemental, just eager and alive. Earnest does have copious quantities of joy and enthusiasm. He loves God and I imagine God loves him a lot.

Grace invited me round for tea tomorrow. 'Just you dear,' she said. 'Let the hungry horde fend for themselves for once.'

Monday 3rd February

I *am* special. Grace says so. She told me not to worry about Sybil Sharpe. There's a Sybil Sharpe in most congregations – dreadful thought – even in missionary societies! You love them and get on with what the Lord wants, and never mind what they say. Came away feeling cared for.

Tuesday 4th February

Retreat with Eucharist this weekend. Maybe I'll be sick.

Wednesday 5th February

Looked at retreat preparation material. Sounds mystical and super spiritual. We are to come with an open mind. That should pose no problem. Mine is so empty it's full of open space. Hope I can hide in the background.

Thursday 6th February

Getting panicky and distracted. Dropped an entire armful of laundry down the loo instead of in the adjacent laundry basket, and sprayed under my arms with hair lacquer. My mind is not on earthly things.

Friday 7th February

What do you pack for a retreat? Should I take my oldest worn 'I am not of this world' clothes or should I try to look smart? Do I need to leave behind worldly trappings like mascara and money? Packed the mascara and my five-piece super volume hair style system with interchangeable brush and tongs, on the basis that it's as well to be prepared for any eventuality. Wondered about putting in our two 'end of Christian conference, acceptably funny but not over the top, avoiding all innuendo, party piece sketches', in case there's a last night concert. Didn't. Packed two large, comfy cushions in case we're meant to sit cross-legged on the floor and intone phrases of Christian truth repetitively. Unpacked them. I think retreats are meant to be about self-denial and unworldliness. And anyway, if we were the only ones with cushions we'd have to give them away to those in greater need. Maybe someone else will come with cushions and be obliged to give them to us in order to look spiritual.

Since we had come a long way, we arrived at the conference centre a bit late for tea. Did the 'smile and nod all round, we are all Christians together and are therefore family, even though we have never met' bit. Tea was one, reheated in the microwave, dehydrated with a crack through the middle, baked potato with a piece of non-conformist Christian pizza – just plain tomato and cheese topping with no fancy extras. First signs of mortification of the flesh. Thankfully the beds are comfortable and the shower has piping hot water, not the Christian conference centre, 'we can't quite afford to heat it beyond lukewarm and anyhow it's good for the soul' kind.

Saturday 8th February

Motley crew assembled for breakfast. (Amazingly good breakfast with croissants and peach preserve and yoghurt.) The lady next to me had a rainbow-coloured kaftan, massive multi-coloured ear-rings and long black hair perilously piled up with hair grips. Thought she was probably an artist; she turned out to be a gynaecologist. The other lady on our table had that 'just returned from missionary service look': crinkled, scrubbed clean, brown face; matted woolly jumper two sizes too small; she was a Scandinavian bishop's wife. The world is full of surprises. Never know how to introduce myself. They knew I was a Rev's wife anyway. Is it that obvious?

Horrors. There are only twenty-five of us here. There is nowhere to hide. Should have brought all my beige, fade-into-the-background clothes.

Very gentle introduction. The leaders told us that the retreat was to provide whatever we personally needed and so we may walk, rest or even sleep. Glorious sense of freedom! What do you do with so much freedom? I am more used to the Christian notion of productivity, meetings and activity. Rest is an alien concept. Took copious notes to make me feel productive.

Today we are to rejoice in creation. Went out and felt leaves and berries and bark. Also felt silly. Passers-by look at you when you are enraptured by a leaf, especially when you are talking to it.

Watched the Eucharist as it approached me, carefully noting what you are meant to do. It's hard to think of Jesus when your mind is so engaged in avoiding the place where the person with the cold, three seats before you, drank from. Maybe it'll be better tomorrow; my ability to be spiritually focused that is, not his cold. Though of course I do hope his cold will be better too.

Sunday 9th February

Food is actually excellent but I couldn't enjoy it fully today. We had a silent lunch so I chose all the 'quietest' food from the buffet table, lest the whole room be amazed by my celery and carrot chewing. I had a plateful of yoghurt, mayonnaise and chocolate cake. Other people's food noises were very distracting, never mind their plate scraping. How do monks handle this every day? Kept my head down. I don't know how to look other people in the eye, keep on munching and not talk to them. We were meant to be praying silently for those whom we looked at. On this basis the chocolate cake was very blessed. Drifted into my own personal day-dream. Got very fixated on the actual eating process and started squishing yoghurt round my mouth like Michael does, feeling its texture and enjoying the slurpy, sucking sounds. Lifted my head in time to see half a dozen people staring at me. Trev tells me I sounded like bath water going down the plug-hole. Completely embarrassed. I want to hide.

I was nearer the beginning of the Eucharist today, thus avoiding the person with the cold. All I had to worry about was getting the 'hold, drink, wipe, pass and reflect' in the right order. And, of course, take care not to drop such a big, heavy cup. Single cups are less stressful. Slept half of the afternoon and only felt slightly guilty. Meditated on a tree root outside the window and thought about my spiritual roots. I am enjoying this.

Monday 10th February

We are to meditate on a fallen world today and look at empty crisp bags and abandoned beer cans as symbols of this. Took a long time to find my first beer can. Set it up on a post and surveyed it. Had some very deep spiritual thoughts about beer cans.

Eucharist was good. Lovely words about God binding up our wounds and our love for God being like mist. I am beginning to feel bound up, but fog might be a more appropriate term for my love.

Tuesday 11th February

I think I am beginning to get the hang of retreating. Walked alone and rolled thoughts of God around in my head. Only one problem today. I climbed over a gate into what I thought was an empty meadow; it wasn't. When I was half way across, a huge stallion appeared out of nowhere. Thought about stopping and commanding it in faith to be still, but ran in abject fear instead, all the way asking God for a mighty deliverance. The horse ran faster. Discovered that horses are really very big close up. Praised God that he had seen fit to put quite a lot of bushes in this particular field, so I could dodge behind them. Though only managed to do the praising bit later. Was forced eventually to scramble through a very small hole in the hedge rather than run across open ground to the gate. This incident seriously interfered with my state of spiritual calm.

Really glad I brought the five-piece super volume hair style system to untangle the bits of hedge from my hair.

Shared dramatically and, I think, most impressively

with the others later, how God makes a way of escape. Found myself preaching Trev's last Sunday's sermon about an *'ekbasis'*, a way of escape. All my good spiritual thoughts seem to be second-hand. Didn't tell them how afraid I was.

Wednesday 12th February

I knew it. The expose-yourself-totally sharing time was bound to come. We have to get into groups of four and say how we have been 'spoken to'. What if we haven't been spoken to? What if there's been a deafening silence from God? Felt pressure to concoct something so I wouldn't be the odd one out. Why can't they leave us in peace to swill around in our own failure?

The beer-can thoughts seem laughable now – all about us being the dregs and God loving us anyway, and how we sometimes get thrown away and crushed yet God valuing even the crushed ones, the bruised reeds and the smoking flax. Bruised reeds and smoking flax sound nicer than trampled beer cans, more poetic and timeless really. Feel like some sort of odd-ball street preacher shouting out, 'I was a crushed beer can and the Lord filled me!' If you said this kind of thing anywhere else they would put you away. Since it was all I had, I said it anyhow. There were a lot of sympathetic, understanding looks and wise, earnest nods at appropriate points. The gynaecologist seemed quite taken with being a beer can. Apparently it reminded her of Jeremiah's pots. We could be reshaped by God and made into something useful, like a coke can. That's definitely more spiritual than a beer can. Maybe if I allowed myself to be completely crushed and re-formed I could become a cup or a jug. A lay-preaching greengrocer wanted to know if I saw myself as the can or the dregs. I don't know really. He prayed for my recycling.

Realised too late that I should have shared the thoughts about our roots going deep or God's love as a mist – they would both have been more spiritual.

Back in my room I prayed that God would use me even if I feel like a crushed can. That he would straighten me out and fill me up with himself. I feel like I'm very full of me. It is amazing that God loves me.

Retreat leaders anointed us with oil this evening and prayed for us individually. I have never been anointed with oil before. Couldn't wait for my turn. God must be in this. They prayed that my cup would be full to overflowing. I am a redeemed can! I am a full cup as well! I feel deeply satisfied with God and full up with him. Please God, let this contentment stay for a little while.

Thursday 13th February

Home today. Michael had prepared tea for us. Stewed rhubarb and thick, lumpy custard with very weak tea. He watched us eat it. Every mouthful. Susannah had done a 'Welcome Home' banner. It's good to be loved. Learned even more about God from this than from the retreat. He delights in his children's imperfect gifts if they're given in love. Or perhaps the retreat has taught me to reflect and take everything in rather than rushing on to the next thing without thinking.

I feel more relaxed than I have in months. Kind of cleaned out and refreshed inside.

Friday 14th February

Val came to see how I'd got on. Told her about the horse and my fear and about the beer can and the roots and the potentially infected communion cup. Says she's never met a Christian like me before. Didn't dare ask her if this was good or bad.

She took care of Billy the goat while we were away. I have become quite fond of him. Seems a bit sad that goats represent the lost. Wonder why! Certainly they seem more rebellious and self-willed. Took the plunge and went for a very brave evangelistic opening. Asked Val if she'd rather be a sheep or a goat. Said she'd like to be a stallion, free to gallop through fields with bushes. Very disappointing. Couldn't think of a single follow-up line to this.

It is very difficult to know when someone's teasing.

Apparently she said to Trev that my honesty was mind-blowing. Should have prepared a more spiritual account of the retreat.

Saturday 15th February

Mountainous pile of laundry. Things as mundane as laundry don't get a mention in Scripture. I will try to be spiritual about laundry. If I can manage it with beer cans then surely nothing is impossible. Remembered 'All our righteousness is like filthy rags' which I translated to 'All the good things I do are as disgusting as smelly socks'. Then thought of 'Cleanse me with hyssop and I shall be clean; wash me, and I shall be whiter than snow'. This could read 'When I use God's special washing powder I will be clean all over'. Very excited about the domestic images in Scripture. Maybe God is calling me to do a housewife's translation of the Bible.

Sunday 16th February

Fellowship hugs are becoming the norm in our church. This is definitely a post-charismatic feature along with hand raising and a worship group. I cannot remember church hugs ten years ago. All kinds of oily-faced, unappealing men are now free to launch themselves at you in full view of their wives. I fear that this may give licence to the lecherous. Sybil Sharpe does not approve of Derek giving hugs. Though when Sybil is not there Derek sprints round the church, up and down both aisles and over the pews like an Olympic hurdler, 'making contact' with all the attractive, single girls and doing the extended length, close embrace, double-cheek version hug. Sybil prefers a firm, Christian handshake. (In my experience most Christian handshakes are of the limp, clammy, wet-fish type or the relentless, priming a pump, with potential dislocated shoulder kind.) Noticed that nobody hugs Mrs Mallusk, a spectacularly hairy-chinned lady. This cannot be biblical.

Wesley seems to be very into church hugs too.

Monday 17th February

Alice and I met Wesley down town today. He gave her a very warm 'Christian hug'. Strange, he doesn't seem to feel the same urge to hug me. Perhaps he feels daunted by the ministry wife image and my towering spirituality.

Tuesday 18th February

Wesley phoned to see if he could come and 'seek spiritual counsel'. He has read a strange article suggesting that the biblical way to find a wife is to go into the desert and sit by a well until God's choice comes to draw water for you and your flocks. This may be difficult in our town. I suggested that the nearest equivalent might be the public drinking fountain by the sand-pit in the children's play park. He did not respond to this idea. He sat by the tap in our kitchen all evening, refusing offers of tea and coffee. Apparently this is God's chosen place for him. Hope God doesn't choose it for too long. Susannah offered him her stuffed toy camel from Israel as a prop. No fair maiden came to offer him and the camel a drink all evening, just me and my kettle, followed by Trev and the dishes. The article's second suggestion was to present approximately 200 foreskins of your intended father-in-law's enemies to him. Maybe sitting by the tap is not so bad after all.

Wednesday 19th February

I am determined to have quiet, reflective time and not let the retreat go to waste. Settled down to assess my life. Flicked through last year's diary and saw all my unfulfilled aims for the year. Need to make a fresh start on both spiritual and general resolutions. I will work on a positive attitude to the criticisers and attackers and not be afraid of them.

On this basis I prayed for Sybil Sharpe and made her a chocolate cake. Feel better about her already. Was too scared to go round with the cake so asked Trev to go. He refused! Says I need to face my own lions in their own den. I prayed very hard for me and nearly ate the chocolate cake myself. Please don't let me be afraid of her, Lord. Decided to be like Elijah and have the food reward after doing battle.

Sybil's house is very neat and very beige. She has photographs of all her personal trophies of grace displayed round the walls of her front room, labelled with dates, places and Scripture verses used, a bit like a big game hunter. Apparently she saved Derek from a life of debauchery (he was under the influence of five cans of shandy a week) and then married him. Her daughter, Lois Eunice Sheba (queen of), was saved from a life of loose living, through Sybil, when she was five.

Apparently Sybil is fasting today but Derek, who 'has not yet reached the path of higher, spiritual disciplines', will be able to eat the cake. She drank water while I had tea and a slice of my own chocolate cake. Found a piece of egg shell in my portion of cake and was forced to scrunch and swallow the evidence of my own culinary ineptitude. Had a second piece in order to personally consume as much rogue egg shell as possible.

Sybil says spiritual disciplines bring discernment. That's how she knows our church is 'not what it once was'. She is fasting from all fleshly things: food, TV and Derek. Derek looked relieved. Don't know whether it was because of the chocolate cake or Sybil fasting from him. He is allowed out to the mid-week meeting on his own tonight.

Shared with her how God blessed me at the retreat and told her I was a redeemed can, straightened out and full of God's blessing. I don't think she likes other people to be blessed. Since the retreat was led by those not of the true church she discerns that it may have been a false blessing and a deception. We are to test the spirits.

'Just like the brandy you've been testing, dear?' said Derek quite innocently.

She turned puce and told him to go to the kitchen and eat his cake there. He may not be allowed out tonight.

Returned to collect my forgotten umbrella. Strange, Sybil seemed to be ingesting something brown and sticky.

Thursday 20th February

Decided to pay a guilt visit to Mrs Mallusk. I am determined to do what is right and what is expected of me
and what any normal ministry wife would do and
what all other ministry wives do and what nobody
else in the congregation would be expected to do.

Why do I panic at the mere thought of drying up in
a parishioner's front room, or being criticised, or Trev
being criticised, or being asked a question I can't
answer? I think I have visitophobia.

Waited till after school so I could take Susannah for
protection, on the principle that I am less likely to be
verbally mauled with children present. Maybe I should
take Michael, Tim and Alice too. Held Susannah's hand
tight. Stood on Mrs Mallusk's front step in terror,
bearing flowers and a smile which did not reflect my
inner state. Considered various conversation openers in
advance. Since she is widowed, has no grandchildren
and does not speak to her daughter there did not appear
to be much on offer. Destined for a complete medical
history. Mrs Mallusk has gall stones, indigestion and
gastric something. She has had these for years and
before that she was laid low with chronic complaint
syndrome. I think she may still have this condition.

I knew we were doomed the minute she got out her
diary. According to her 'meticulous, personal
records', no one from the church has called to visit her
for the last 163 days and the pastor has not been in her
home for 297 days. His chats after 'The Senior
Citizens' meeting and his friendly enquiries at church
do not count. This record is a disgrace and Mrs

Mallusk intends to see that something is done about it. I had to restrain myself from saying, 'Nobody calls because you are such an unpleasant old bat. You spend your whole life complaining. You have nothing genuinely wrong with you. There are others in much greater need. Nobody likes you and your super-hairy chin makes me think of the witch in Hansel and Gretel.' I could feel my teacup rattling nervously in its saucer at the prospect. Sometimes I think too much submission and restraint makes it increasingly likely that my top will blow some day and I'll scream dreadful, though truthful, abuse at all unkind, thoughtless, demanding and self-satisfied church members. Wonder what the outcome would be if we had a total truth-telling day at church?

As a first course of action, Mrs Mallusk is removing her covenant of two pounds a month and she will be in contact with the office bearers to make sure they all know that the level of pastoral care is unacceptable. Susannah's helpful comment that tomorrow she would be able to say, 'No one from this church has visited me for one day,' did not go down well.

Must remind Trev to wear his armour plating when he calls.

Felt quite giddy tonight. I think it is post-difficult-visit relief.

Friday 21st February

I *must* find my spiritual gift. If I did this I would not have to visit Mrs Mallusk or anyone else ever again, since I would officially discover, and be able to anounce to the church, that I am not equipped by God to visit. Urged Trev to send away for an American course which works out your spiritual gifts in eight easy lessons. It would be one hundred and ten pounds well spent!

Trev actually agreed to send for the course. He must feel threatened like me.

Saturday 22nd February

Billy the goat clearly knows what kind of a home he's come to and what Christians ought to be about. This morning he was spotted reaching out to our neighbours, in fact he reached out right through the fence and helped himself to a generous mouthful of snowdrops. This was not his first attempt at cross-cultural evangelism. Last week he made personal contact with the neighbours on the other side who are of Asian extraction, eating just a few items of clothing from their washing line. For his earnest commitment to reach out to all nations, we have decided to rename him. From henceforth he is no longer Billy the goat but Billy Graham.

Sunday 23rd February

Wesley sat beside us in church this morning. His desire for close fellowship is obviously very deep. After every hymn, he seemed to creep a little nearer when he sat down. Alice, who was next to him, looked extremely uncomfortable and worried and kept shuffling closer and closer to me. By the third hymn I was strait-jacketed between Alice and the pew end and having serious difficulty drawing breath, and Alice was a shade of red I have never seen her before. Wesley was in a state of excited euphoria and was even pinker than usual. At this rate, the descent after the praise time had all the potential of lateral pressure shooting me forward like a cork out of a bottle or crushing me to death.

When Trev encouraged us to greet one another I knew what was coming. I half whispered urgently to Alice, 'Stand.' She leapt up, Wesley rocketed into me, his kiss hit my cheek instead of Alice's and half a dozen very responsive and obedient members nearby automatically stood up too and looked to me for further instructions. Trev looked very puzzled.

'I sense God is telling us to move around and greet those who don't usually sit near us,' I said. Then in a moment of divine inspiration. 'In fact I think he is saying we should change seats completely for this Sunday and have fellowship with those we don't know so well.' I grabbed Alice and my things and made for the furthermost reaches of the church. The 'this has been my pew for the last thirty years and given the chance I would like to die in it' group were not pleased. I thought they might start a chorus of 'We shall not, we shall not be moved'. But they used the loud, meant-to-be-overheard, negative comments, timed for maximum effect in front of everybody else, in a full porch, after-church technique, instead.

Mavis breezed up to me afterwards full of wonder that the Lord should speak so directly to me during the service. I was most grateful for his clear guidance too. She feels I am moving into a period of more complete sensitivity to him. I do hope so.

Trev needs to have a serious word with Wesley.

Monday 24th February

Trev in London for Spring Onion preparation day. Couldn't wait to hear about all the Christian VIPs. He will be rubbing shoulders with lots of big-name speakers. Prayed that he would be accepted and blessed and encouraged. Trev is every bit as gifted as they are so why are they more famous? Wonder if they feel ordinary too? He brought back lots of interesting information: they all seem to know each other, one of Britain's key Christian leaders picks his nose and a very big-name speaker has bad breath. At least Trev got close enough to detect it. Trev is to take a seminar on 'Signs and Wonders'. This is rather worrying since we have never experienced any. Urgent prayer needed.

'Please God, send us a wonder or a sign, definitely before Spring Onion. Then we can decide whether they are really from you. I suppose if you answer this prayer and send one, then that means they must be from you. On the other hand, now we've asked for one, maybe that opens us up to a satanic counterfeit or self-deception. Perhaps it's better not to have had the actual experience, but to decide from a position of personal ignorance, like many Christians do; the way non-Christians say there's no God because they haven't experienced you.

I realise experience is no basis on which to judge, at least not on its own, but why then do we put so much stress on a conversion experience? And since there were signs and wonders and gifts in Scripture, that should be enough, shouldn't it? And are signs and wonders just gifts, but even more so?

I think a lot of Christians don't really want there to be signs or wonders or gifts because it's scary when something outside your control happens. And most of us like to be in control and even make churches go the way we want personally. Inside we think, 'Never mind God. Let him get on with something else and keep his miracle-working hands off our church, thank you very much!'

I would really like there to be some signs and gifts, since they would be very helpful, and it seems right that a father should give gifts. But since I haven't received any, at least not the spectacular kind, then maybe it's safest just to say there are none. That seems the most straightforward option. And a lot of people would applaud us as being 'sound'.

We are open, just in case you have anything to give. I'm not quite sure if I've actually asked for anything, but if I have, please answer. And I don't want to have you all wrapped up in my own safe, limited box. Thank you for dealing with very confused people like me and their very confusing prayers. Amen.

Felt better after this and kind of safe in God. Wonder if he'll do anything.

Tuesday 25th February

Assaulted by monthly 'symptoms' again. PMS sort of creeps up on me. I gradually become more and more tetchy and then eventually slide into a black pit of despair and aggravation. First signs today. Am determined that this month I will *not* lose my Christian witness. Overheard Trev on the phone to Dave saying it was 'Fasten on your tin helmet time', then Tim asked me if I'd like any Evening Primrose Oil. Didn't know whether to say, 'Thank you, most sensitive son,' or, 'How dare you, this is your mother you're speaking to!' Is it that obvious anyway? I suppose he *was* trying to catch the marmalade jar and the butter dish I'd thrown at him, at the time. But men are particularly frustrating at this time of the month. Trev says it's time I did something about the PMS. What am I supposed to do? God gave me the rotten hormones so it's his problem, not mine. Currently, I cannot imagine any possible human solution. Why is there nothing in the Bible about PMS or hormones for that matter? Looked up a concordance. Tried 'mood', 'despair', 'menstruation', 'hopelessness', 'anxiety' and 'crying'. Levitical references most discouraging. I will try the Christian bookshop later this week.

Wednesday 26th February

Too weepy to go out. Yelled at Susannah for leaving her room in a mess and kicked Billy Graham while he was quietly munching his breakfast. PMS is like an appendix; it serves no useful purpose. Did God intend it? If not, then surely I can claim victory over it? This would be a good time for a sign or a wonder. Commanded the PMS to go. It didn't. I have been singularly unsuccessful in commanding so far, having tried galloping horses and PMS. Maybe this is what deliverance ministry is for. Don't know any deliverers except God himself. Asked God to deliver me from PMS.

Thursday 27th February

Went to the Christian bookshop and asked if there was anything on PMS. The young, wet behind the ears, male assistant said knowingly, 'Oh yes, Post Modern Society. Back left, behind Schaeffer and Ravi Zacharias.'

'No,' I shouted, 'It does *not* mean Post Modern Society.' (Secretly flattered that I looked intelligent enough to know about such things.)

'No, no, of course not. You want Pre Millennial Systems or,' with a smile, and a knowing, all-things-to-all-men nod, 'perhaps Post Millennial Systems – depending on where you're standing, madam.'

'I am standing in a Christian bookshop,' I cried, 'and I want Premenstrual Syndrome. Or rather I do *not* want Premenstrual Syndrome, but I've got it whether I want it or not. Do I have to spell it out? I need practical, biblical help with a pressing female problem.'

'If you wait a moment, I'll just get my mother,' he said, and fled.

Clearly men are out of their depth here.

Came home with a mine of personal strategies from a woman of some experience. I am to reduce my tea, coffee and salt intake, eliminate dairy produce and wheat-based products and make sure I go no longer than three hours without carbohydrates. Is life worth living without cheese on toast? I think this qualifies as deliverance though.

Also came home with a new Bible study method called *How to Read God's Word to Hear God Speak*. It sounds exactly what I need. I am finished with coloured pencils.

Friday 28th February

Brilliant Bible study time! God is there! Even in obscure Old Testament passages. I worked through a bit of Genesis all about kings and people getting stuck in tar pits and it was so real! Thank you, God, that you spoke to me. I really do love you, God. I am open to hear from you and I'm going to be like Abraham, ready to let everything go.

Saturday 1st March

Didn't think God was going to ask me to let the car go and the full no-claim bonus too! Isn't he meant to protect his saints when they're engaged in spiritual activities, and keep cars safe, just like in Frank Peretti's books?

Trev made a full-frontal attack on a new Peugeot in a slow-moving traffic queue. He's so keen on conversation with eye contact that his head operates on a constant swivel basis, even while driving. He would have been happy with a neck like ET's. The lady whose rear he attacked is making a full claim. Really glad we don't have a 'Carpenter from Nazareth Seeks Joiners' or a 'Follow Me, I'm Following the Master' sign stuck to the car and that Trev wasn't wearing his ring of confidence. The Peugeot had 'I'm Out for a Good Time' stuck on its back window. Is there no justice?

Is this God testing us or Satan's attack? Or is there another category called human frailty, or your own fault? Tried to tell Trev that it didn't matter, that God would take care of it. He looked so forlorn and lost. Prayed for him and gave him a relaxing massage. Susannah and Michael offered all the money from their money-boxes. Thank you for such loving kids.

Sunday 2nd March

It's tough having to preach and sound full of hope when it's the last thing you feel like. Preachers need 'crawl into a corner and be left alone' days too; instead they have to be super-smiley Christians, full of joy and victory all the time.

Trev parked the car half way into the hedge in the church car park to hide it from church members. Didn't work. They gathered round it like bees, patting it and muttering about bodywork.

How can I move from such encouragement to such discouragement in less than twenty-four hours? Am I so circumstance dependent? Prayed that God would lift our spirits and help us believe the 'All things work together for good' bit.

Monday 3rd March

We have £1,500 worth of crunch damage, plus £500 for the other car. Thank goodness for insurance companies.

No car today so I had to walk to the local shops. Encountered the check-out girl who wanted a mystical experience; hoped she had forgotten. She hadn't.

'Oh yes,' she said in a kind of breathy whisper, 'You're the one who wears white robes and has rituals in the garden. I'm into the paranormal too, you know. I'm really, really interested.'

I think it was God who invited her round for coffee, it certainly wasn't me.

Tuesday 4th March

What am I going to say to her? Phoned Val. She said, 'Just ask her about goats and sheep. That should go down well. Though if she's into stuff like that, she probably wants to be a frog or a bat.' Honestly, God, why don't you do your own evangelism?

Wednesday 5th March

Not sure why I phoned Val in the first place, I mean she's not one of *us* yet. It's very hard to think of people just as people. I mean they're not really people; they're either in or out, Christians or non-Christians, saved or lost! *They* think of themselves as non-church-goers, or non-religious, or C of E for purposes of weddings and funerals, or British and therefore Christian. We just think of 'them' and 'us'.

Thursday 6th March

Prayed round every room of the house, against satanic influence; you never know what Aurora will bring with her.

Friday 7th March

Aurora takes herbal tea and likes to sit facing the east. She detected spiritual influences in our house. That's a relief!

I was just bringing the conversation round to Jesus, ever so slowly and tactfully and indirectly and care-fully and without offence and praying inwardly for guidance and that the Spirit would prepare the way, when Val arrived. Felt like saying, 'Nothing today thank you,' and closing the door. Made a lot of 'Really, I'm very busy at the moment, it would be better if you called another time' comments, but Val pushed on down the hall, leaving me standing by the front door. Honestly, sometimes non-Christians have even fewer manners than Christians. Got myself psyched up for deep spiritual warfare. I had never seen such a clear example of Satan's sabotage and hindrance. Stopped in my tracks when Val started talking to Aurora about needing to find God himself, not just mystical, spiritual feelings. I had to hold onto the distressed tables. Could feel my eyes widen and my jaw drop further and further. Didn't realise quite how much Val had been taking in over the last months at church.

'No point beating about the bush,' she said, 'the plain truth is that we need a relationship with God. Nothing else will do. You can play spiritual games but the bottom line is, we need forgiveness and love and acceptance. Look Liz, you're so careful not to sound like some religious crank that you tend to talk round the issue. Aurora can listen while you take me through the stuff. I've heard enough and seen enough to know it's true.' I rambled incoherently through verses, trying to put together some kind of picture of a Father who loves us and wants us so much.

Val prayed, 'Dear God, I really need you. Please forgive me for all my rotten past. Thank you for coming just for me and I'm even willing to be a sheep or a lamb rather than a goat, whatever it takes, just have me in your family, please. Teach me the right way from now on. Yours sincerely, Val.' And that was that! Realised again that God likes to do things in his own way.

God, please keep her from the evangelical sausage machine.

Saturday 8th March

Wondered if Val was a sign or a wonder. Maybe she's a gift.

Sunday 9th March

Aurora and Val came to church today. I could see it was an alien experience for Aurora. Prayed that she would encounter the real Jesus despite the time warp of hymn language. 'Pavilioned in splendour and girded with praise' doesn't mean much when the only pavilion you know is in Brighton and 'girded' suggests something uncomfortably elasticated for middle-age spread. Rivers which keep your feet dancing aren't much better either. I suspect she felt much as I would in a bingo hall – out of place and very self-conscious.

A lot of people hugged Val. Hoped Aurora wouldn't feel left out. Sent Tim and Michael to corner Wesley Tweed so he wouldn't get to her. Thankfully, Grace and Earnest took Aurora and Val home for lunch.

Monday 10th March

Am I an evangelist? Asked Trev this at lunch today. He said, 'One egg sandwich doesn't make a church supper.' Didn't quite follow him.

Tuesday 11th March

Women's meeting tonight. Not sure if it's safe to take Val, might be even more of a culture shock than the Sunday service. Tonight it's a special guest soloist and a talk on 'The lifestyle values of TV soaps'. Dangerous territory with a female audience. Huge guilt-inducing potential.

Amazing performance from the great, glass-shattering voiced soloist with the almost obligatory 'How great thou art'. Unfortunately, just after she started singing, a mouse appeared on the platform beside her. Ada Hemp, her trusty accompanist, went relentlessly battering on in a life or death struggle with the three flats required to produce harmony. It was a myopic, eyeball-to-eyeball encounter with the sheet music, so she failed to hear the plaintive, shrill cries for help, or see the demented antics of the soloist. During the course of her 'ministry in song' she turned and faced the side wall, eyes fastened constantly on the mouse (which had wandered innocently to the shelter of the radiator), shuffled around looking ever more desperate, stared fixedly at the floor, climbed up on a chair, abandoning the microphone (which nobody in their right mind should have given her in the first place) and then eventually stood facing the wall behind her, where the mouse had finally settled, for the final ear-splitting crescendo. Since no one except those in the front row could see the mouse, the rest of the ladies clearly thought she had gone out of her mind. To their absolute amazement she kept singing in extra bits as she went along like:

Oh Lord my God, (Oh no!)
When I in awsome wonder (Go away)
Consider all (Clear off)
The works Thy hand hath made. (Cats, cats!)
I see the trees (Oh horrors!)
I hear the mighty thunder, (Scram)
Thy power throughout the universe displayed.
    (Get me out of here.)

The pitch got higher and higher, and those in the front row, who could see, were paralytic with laughter.

I don't think she will be returning to our women's meeting.

The excellently prepared talk was somewhat of an anti-climax.

Wednesday 12th March

Perhaps I have the gift of teaching. Because of potentially injurious family comment, I was forced to assess this gift in the only place of privacy in our house, the bathroom. Tried out a few sermonic poses in front of the bathroom mirror. The tilted head is most effective (a thoughtful, authoritative pose indicating considered judgement), as is the removal of the reading glasses, holding them with studied nonchalance, while fixing the congregation with a meaningful gaze. This is best accompanied by an equally meaningful pause. Tried a bit of thundering and dramatic pacing up and down, though there wasn't really enough room to get going because of the Ali Baba laundry basket. Used this as my pulpit and kept returning to it to establish my authority. Finished with a studious turn to my notes (a copy of the *National Geographic*, strategically placed, in normal British fashion, where it may provide enlightenment to those unavoidably detained in this area). I think notes waved in the air should be used sparingly, it looked much too showy in the mirror.

All I have to work on now is the right voice and, of course, the content. I feel there is definite promise here.

Trev reminded me that content may need a few years or so of preparation in Bible college. I had forgotten this. I am not sure I want the gift of teaching; it seems like a lot of hard work. Maybe God will give me the words to speak without the preparation. Lots of speakers I have heard seem to work on this principle.

Thursday 13th March

I knew it. I have the gift of faith. Exercised it this morning. I believed that Alice would be first into the bathroom, and she was; then I believed for a phone call from a member of the congregation and it came. This is really exciting. I will exercise faith for deliverance from PMS. Told Trev I couldn't wait till next PMS time, that I was exercising faith. He said he'd rather not wait for it either. Then had faith for Aurora's salvation. Strengthened my faith by saying, 'She will believe, she will believe, she will believe,' twenty-five times on the basis that we are to speak out words of faith.

Heard Trev on the phone to Dave talking about an early menopause. I don't think there is such a thing as a male menopause, so he needn't worry. Anyhow, he's much too young. When he came off the phone I offered to pray for him in faith about the menopause too, but he said it had been a hard day and he just wanted to go to bed early and forget it all.

Friday 14th March

Wesley Tweed called, just to smile, I think.

Saturday 15th March

Exercised faith for a sign today. Since I need a sign to confirm my teaching gift, I will expect a phone call with an invitation to speak at a significant Christian event. No sign, unless the request for a loaf of egg sandwiches (without onion) for the Senior Citizens' meeting counts. Spent most of the day urging Michael through reflexive French verbs and encouraging Susannah to tidy her bedroom. Real life is very ordinary.

Sunday 16th March

Val came to both services. She's so eager to learn and she's really my total, personal responsibility. Tried to show her around the Bible a bit and help her find the right place. Hoped the sermon would be in the New Testament since I can find things there easily. Anything in the Old Testament beyond Daniel is stepping out into a great void. I just open at random and hope for the best. It was Nahum; bang in the middle of the minor unknowns. Showed Val where the index was, so if *she* was ever unsure she would know where to go and assured her that soon she'd be leaping around Scripture with confidence, just like the rest of us. I will have to memorise the second half of the Old Testament before next Sunday.

Monday 17th March

Trev got a hand-delivered 'Dear John' letter today. Another indication of thoughtful timing by one of our caring members, just designed to brighten up Trev's day off.

They always begin in much the same way, 'Dear Pastor, It is with considerable sadness that I pen these words to you' – just in case you should have ripped open the envelope too enthusiastically and started reading with the vague hope that it might be a 'Thank you for all your hard work among us' note and that a cheque might even flutter out from its pages of encouraging discourse.

This one followed the classic pattern well established for every pastoral discourager, and used the 'How to rattle your pastor's cage' basic letter layout and suggested content, as described in that much read congregational magazine *From Pew to Pulpit*.

Dear Pastor,

It is with regret and sadness that I write to you, but following this past Sunday's services, I feel I have no choice but to express my concern for the church of which I have been a member for over thirty-five years.

You, as Pastor, are merely a bird of passage; it is we who own this church and indeed, I might add, the manse. Enough said.

If matters are not taken in hand and the slide into charismatic and liberal error stopped immediately, then I will be forced to bring this matter to a public meeting, specially convened under article 14b, sub section (iii) of our constitution 'How to get rid of a pastor'.

Writing this letter has been painful for me, but I can no longer remain silent. The movement away from our historic faith, once delivered to the saints, and its replacement with what can only be termed a jamboree with guitars and drums, is unacceptable not only to myself but to many others in our congregation. If an organ was good enough for the early church, then it is more than good enough for me.

I object most strongly to the use of tuneless and inane modern songs. Let us go back to the hymns which have stood the test of time, great words like 'We shall see one another clearly when the mists are rolled away', and 'Do you want a pilot, signal then to Jesus'. Bring back Moody and Sankey. Hand clapping and hand raising are signs of a frothy and superficial faith. Worship is a serious affair and not a party or some kind of celebration. God does not wish us to be happy here and now. Remember, we are not of this world.

I notice, too, that women are now taking public part in our services and the proper place of men as those placed in authority seems to be under threat. When am *I* going to be asked to speak to the assembly, is what I would like to know?

There is, I note, increasing reference to the Holy Spirit in your preaching. The Holy Spirit has always had his proper place in this church, and he does not need any help from you. We do not need any more of the Holy Spirit. I, personally, have quite enough, thank you. We are a Bible-based church, noted for our focus on the word of God. The word is all we need.

Added to this is the fact that pastoral visitation is not what it was under our former pastor. I was not visited when I had a blister on my big toe last month and last year no one called to invite me to the fellowship Christmas party, which in any case I disapprove of.

I want you to know that I am not alone in my thinking. I have discussed these matters with a number of members in our fellowship, in your absence, and many are of like mind.

I wish this letter to be read in full, both at the office-bearers' meeting and at the church business meeting next week, when I intend being present to explain the biblical position more fully to those like yourself who walk in error, and to discredit those who disagree.

Of course, I do all of this in love for the brethren, and for your refining.

Remember, you are not indispensable.
Yours for truth and judgement
Duncan Woodnot.

Prayed for Mr Woodnot.
Coffee and cake in 'The Cosy Cup' tasted like dirty dishwater and dry All Bran after a letter like that. Horrible sick feeling. Trev and I talked about the letter all day.

Tuesday 18th March

Talked about the letter again. Feel threatened and afraid.

Wednesday 19th March

Trev called on Mr Woodnot. He is subtle, self-righteous and smooth and wields his Bible like a toma-hawk missile. He has been spreading poison behind the scenes about Trev; a phone call here, a little comment there. Would like God to send him a per-sonal thunderbolt. Forgiveness is very hard. I will not think about it, I will let God deal with it.

Thursday 20th March

Thought about it again. Made myself pray blessing on Mr Woodnot. I do not feel like he deserves a blessing, but then neither do I.

Friday 21st March

Who would be a pastor? I would like Trev to be a teacher or a bank official or a window cleaner, anything but a pastor. Maybe he won't be a pastor after next Wednesday.

God, please nuke Mr Woodnot before the church business meeting. God, please forgive me for asking you to nuke Mr Woodnot, just lay him aside on a bed of sickness for a while. A long while, please.

Saturday 22nd March

Grace and Earnest called. I cried. Told them I think Trev and I should minister in Africa or South-east Asia or the moon. Anywhere but here. They always say the right thing. No 'All things work together for good' appropriate Scripture verses that you know already. They hugged us and prayed for strength and grace and that we wouldn't waste the experience of criticism. They told us they loved us and that we're not alone. Cried again.

Sunday 23rd March

I do not want to go to church today. Anybody in their right mind would hide in a corner and die. Why can't God give me a suitably impressive and sympathy-gaining illness; nothing too painful, just enough to induce compassion and understanding, so church members would think Mr Woodnot most unkind to attack Trev while his wife is so ill. I would be plied with flasks of hot soup and tempting casseroles, sent flowers and cards, instead of having to come to church and smile and see them whisper together in church porches and car parks and pews. God, help me not to do what they do. Help me to keep my mouth shut and let you handle it. Don't know how Trev preached. Mr Woodnot made copious notes all through the sermon. Watched him afterwards; he talked to Mrs Mallusk, Sybil Sharpe and all the malcontents and potential trouble-makers. God, this is your church, please keep it that way. It's not ours or theirs. A lot of people said quietly they were praying for us. Do they know or are you at work supernaturally, God?

The kids know something's up. God, I want a circle of protection round them right now, like the Colgate ring of confidence only a lot stronger. Had a good idea, we will be like Joshua and the children of Israel. Marched Trev and the kids all round the outside of our house seven times, speaking verses of victory and strength, though Tim refused to sound his trumpet. The woman across the street looked very concerned and Tim looked embarrassed, but we all feel much better now. Boldly asked God for a sign. We really need one now.

Maybe technically we should have marched round the enemy's house, but Mr Woodnot would not understand!

Thank you that we're not alone. We will not fear what man can do to us.

Pris Priddle called with a cake. Is this the sign? Must be feeling better; it tasted like cake, not All Bran.

Monday 24th March

More than anything else in the whole world, I hate contentious church business meetings. They feel like firing squads with Trev as the victim. I am scared silly about what 'they' might say. Please God, make me either very ill so I don't have to go, or very strong so I can handle the unkind comments.

Please God, let me die before Wednesday.

The woman across the street invited Susannah in for lemonade and biscuits, after school. She said she'd seen us running round the house and shouting things. Was this some kind of game and were we all right? Susannah said we were being strong in the Lord and claiming the victory. Don't think she was any the wiser.

Tuesday 25th March

I don't know any other job in the whole world where a hundred or so people can say what they like about you to each other and to your face, criticise you unfairly, tear you apart in public, make unreasonable demands on your time and energy, not pay you enough to provide for your family and then expect you to serve and love and nurture them without reservation as if nothing had happened.

Looked in the Situations Vacant pages for Trev.

Wednesday 26th March

Neither of us could eat anything today. Mitzi called and prayed with me.

God, where are you?

Duncan Woodnot's letter was read out. Thought I was going to faint with fear. Much discussion about where we are going as a church. Attackers very vociferous and very personal. How can Christians speak that way? Don't they realise Trev is a human being with feelings. Then, one by one, the quiet, fearful, tentative, not-wanting-to-cause-trouble, gracious people spoke. They like the worship, they have been blessed by the preaching, and Trev has counselled them through deep, personal difficulties. They realise he's not perfect, but they don't expect him to be.

Trev was brilliant; wise, caring, gracious and clearly seen to be leading.

Feel battered but also relieved. Thank you, God; I know it doesn't always end like this.

Thursday 27th March

Duncan Woodnot's letter of resignation came today; full of vitriol and Scripture.

Friday 28th March

Mitzi took me out today. Kind of post-church-meeting recovery.

She says we need comfort food, replenishing friends, mental and physical distractions and quietness to listen to God, like Elijah after doing battle with the prophets of Baal. She has arranged for the four of us to play badminton tonight and we are being taken to a pizza restaurant afterwards. I don't exactly recall Elijah playing badminton and eating pizza, but it sounds wonderful anyway. Thank God for good friends.

Saturday 29th March

Noticed Duncan Woodnot's name in the church membership roll today. Took a big, blue felt-tip pen, then a big red felt-tip pen and then a symbolic big black felt-tip pen and removed it – thoroughly. Felt much better after this. I'm sure he'll be an asset somewhere but thank you, Lord, that it's no longer here. Then thought about his name being in the Lamb's book of life where I couldn't remove it, and having to share heaven with him. Still, it should be a big enough place to avoid each other.

Took the kids out today for a Big Mac, to celebrate God's love for us and just to be together. Susannah wanted to know if the Woodnot man would be in heaven and if he was a bad man because he tried to get rid of her dad. She obviously has the same problems with God's mercy as I do: I'd like it wide enough for me but not too wide.

Read a helpful quote today, something like 'If you

think your enemies are God's enemies, then you've too small a view of God'.

Sunday 30th March

Trev has definite gifts of peacemaking. I don't know anybody more gracious. Overheard him warding off another nasty SS comment with gentleness. Maybe that's what pastors are for – just catching verbal garbage and not recycling it.

Only a week left to prepare for Spring Onion. Hope Trev has a sign before then. Why did God let all this trouble happen when we needed calm and time to get ready?

Asked Ned what he thought pastors were for. He thought for a moment then said, 'I suppose they're to give us someone to blame.'

Monday 31st March

Prayed for my enemies today. Problem with this is that it brings them to the forefront of your mind just when you'd managed to forget them. How is it possible to forget and forgive at the same time? A miracle is needed.

Another problem is *what* you pray for. Dear heavenly Father please forgive/deal with as you see fit/touch/change/bless/discipline/reveal the true nature of/pour your love on/sear the conscience of/smite with a deadly and painful disease/Mr

Woodnot. The possibilities are endless. Was forced on biblical principle to go for 'bless'. Tried to mean it.

Tuesday 1st April

Spring Onion just a week away and I am not remotely ready spiritually.

Wednesday 2nd April

Mid-week meeting like the calm after the storm. We prayed a lot for 'Those known to you, Lord, who are disaffected and angry'. Everybody knows that everybody else knows that they are known to us too. But we all pretend that we don't know. Nobody ever mentions any names. I am not sure why this is.

Thursday 3rd April

Prayed again for Sybil Sharpe and Derek, Mrs Mallusk and Duncan Woodnot. Secretly wish they'd *all* leave. Why stay in a church when you're not happy? Maybe they'd not be happy anywhere. Wonder if they'll find heaven satisfactory. Church would be great if it weren't for the Christians!

Maybe I should organise a public meeting in town in a neutral venue, for all those from every denomination who are dissatisfied with their minister. Thousands would turn up! I would not of course be there, but knowing their propensity to find fault, they would be enjoying themselves so much complaining, they would hardly notice the lack of an organiser. I think they would fight their way to forming a committee, argue over doctrinal niceties, appoint some unsuspecting human target as their minister and change him every time they put out the rubbish. They could form the Church of the Malcontents and leave the rest of us in peace.

Mitzi phoned me up with a great joke about a chain letter.

Dear church member,

This letter has crossed several countries and continents and has been used of God to do wonderful things. It will bring blessing to you and your church. Within three days you should send copies of this letter to six other churches and post your minister to the first address on the list. After one month you will receive 60,466,176 ministers, from which you should be able to find one who is satisfactory. If you break this chain you will receive your own minister back.

Friday 4th April

I need a total break from our church, just to put 'the current situation' out of my mind and learn to worship without worry again. Anyhow, I can't wait any longer for a close encounter with God. Now is the time for a new adventure in faith. I am going to the local fully charismatic church this Sunday. It is time for ministry and blessing and reaching out to God for new things. Mitzi is going to come with me, just in case anything supernatural should actually happen, both as a witness to any great acts of God that we might experience and also for me to hide behind. It is possible that she may also be needed to catch me.

Don't really know what to tell Val about my defection. Feel really guilty about leaving Trev after the events of last week but maybe I'll be able to bring him back a blessing; apparently they're highly transportable but only if you travel to the place of origin in person.

Saturday 5th April

Had an unfortunate accident today. The tightly bound bundle of four, six-foot curtain poles dislodged themselves from their resting place (probably their last resting place since they have been there awaiting ministerial attention for at least the last eight months), propped up against the kitchen wall, and landed on my head. Direct hit. Trev rescued me from a dazed trance. Heard him telling Dave that I had been 'Touched from above, in a supernatural way. In fact it was nearly curtains for her. She was right in pole position', followed by the typical male laugh that says, 'Women! Honestly!' Any slight feelings of guilt I might have had in defecting to another place of worship this Sunday are now no more. I will leave

Trev to speak to Val. Must think about a disguise for tomorrow. I will have to go incognito.

Sunday 6th April

Decided against the headscarf. Went for the very bright red lipstick, heavy blue eye shadow and blusher, one of Mitzi's short skirts and no Bible. I do not want to look like a Christian in need of a word, nor will I be expected to speak in tongues with such an evidently unredeemed appearance. Whatever happens though I mustn't fall down now, either back-wards or forwards. Mitzi thought I had overdone it. She said she was glad we weren't going on a Saturday night. Didn't understand, but she wouldn't tell me what she meant by this comment. There was a great deal of banner waving going on, and it sounded as though they had been praising for some time, even though we arrived a good five minutes before the appointed time. Most peculiar. Do they not start with a hymn at 11 am precisely, in well-ordered fashion, like the rest of us? Tried to find an unobtrusive seat and carefully avoided the end of a row in case some well-meaning charismatic should want to lay hands on us. Wondered what the blankets at the front were for.

Preaching was better than I anticipated, though nothing of course compared to Trev's. Began to feel quite safe and was looking forward to the time of min-istry at the end, to see what they might get up to. Wasn't disappointed; they had the full charismatic range: tongues and words of knowledge and some prophecies. Hoped I might see someone I knew so I could check for accurate prediction rating later. Though I did not want anyone to recognise me. As soon as folk began falling I discovered what the blankets were for. At least charismatics are concerned for modesty.

The leader had this uncanny knowledge of what was wrong with people (I don't think Sybil Sharpe would approve of this intimate knowledge of other people's bodies), and called them up for prayer. It was really quite exciting; sore backs touched and ears breathed into. I almost wished I had worn more suitable clothes and could go forward for something, when the pastor said, 'There's someone here who desperately wants to know what their spiritual gift is. Please come forward for prayer, I believe we have a word of knowledge for you.' Mitzi said, 'That's you, go on!' Incredible numbness and disbelief. Couldn't go up wearing the dreadfully short skirt, and couldn't risk being seen playing truant from our own church, but so wanted to have my spiritual gift delivered supernaturally, without the usual striving and work. Agony of indecision. What would Trev think if I went forward? What would God think if I didn't? What would our own congregation think if they found out I'd been here in the first place?

Stood up and grabbed Mitzi as a kind of modesty shield and identity protector. 'Whatever you do, stand behind me.' I muttered. The pastor spoke very gently and said I had gifts of mercy, leadership and encouragement. Wow, three gifts in one day! Didn't fall back-wards though. Just sensed a warm glow and my right hand started to shake as if it had a life of its own. Even managed to forget the watching congregation. I felt like I had encountered Jesus and he had personally gift-wrapped a package just for me. 'The Holy Spirit is moving in your life,' said the pastor, 'Just let him have his rightful place.'

Wow and double wow! I have discovered the Holy Spirit, though I know he was always there. It's just that he's so real now. I'm not sure if I'm allowed to tell anybody. Hope Trev understands.

Felt like jumping up and down in our church tonight but didn't dare.

Monday 7th April

Feel ready for anything now. Would like to lay hands on Trev. Didn't dare suggest it to him, though I must confess I wondered if I should do it while he was asleep last nght. Put my hands gently on his head and prayed into myself that the Lord would deeply touch him. He did sort of groan, which I am assured is a good sign, but then again, he started snoring almost immediately. Will wait to see if there is any change.

Tuesday 8th April

Travelled to Spring Onion this morning. Can't wait to lay hands on someone.

We are VIP Christians at last! Maybe this is our

reward for enduring all things. Had to arrive earlier than the general populace, got a special speaker's pack, food tokens, a more up-market chalet *and* a TEAM mug. Wish I had a china cabinet.

Disappointed that the chalet didn't have the usual mildewed walls and the peculiar, ancient sick smell in the carpet. Spring Onion won't be the same without having to disinfect every surface before use.

Wednesday 9th April

No gentle stroll to meetings this year with optional omission of the potentially boring bits and cups of coffee with friends. This is a serious 9 am till 11 pm working week, but then we Christian VIPs are here to serve.

First morning is the usual mass-orienteering event of the year, thousands out in all-weather gear, each with a map of the site turned to align with current position. Couples stand at corners, heads bowed, considering the shortest route between the Palladium and Little Springers, or wander forlornly round and round the outside of buildings looking for a way in. Plotted my course in advance, working out the shortest path between home base (Chalet Z19) and Susannah's destination in Chatterbox at The Gaiety, thence to The Hippodrome with Michael, onwards to the morning Bible reading in Showboat, then to the TEAM lounge in Aviemore for coffee, meeting Alice en route at the corner between Gleneagles and Baps'n'Burgers at 11.15 am precisely, onwards to Trev's first main seminar at Variety Bandstand then back for lunch at the chalet. They ought to give out pedometers and award points and prizes for the most miles clocked up in a Spring Onion week!

Lunch-time; feel well fed spiritually already.

Changed into trainers and jogging bottoms after lunch-time. Added an umbrella and a rucksack to my kit, to hold all Bibles, notebooks and daily newsheets. Wondered about a thermos flask of hot soup in case of total geographical disorientation.

Then inspiration hit – had my best ever Spring Onion idea: speed walking. Thought I'd try out the kind they do as an actual Olympic sport. It involves sort of rolling your hips and shoulders in an exaggerated manner and actually takes quite a bit of practice, but I did have the whole length of the site to get it right. Susannah and Michael refused to walk with me. It was rather unfortunate that I met a very eager member of the counselling team while I was doing this. Explained that I was in a hurry because I was Trev's wife and therefore a Christian with a lot on, and made a joke about the 'Christian walk'. He nodded very seriously and said that if I was in such a rush to get away from Trev that I might find the seminar entitled 'Communication in Marriage' helpful and that there was also a time of prayer for healing in the Starburst Ballroom. I could have hands laid on me there rather than face a double hip replacement operation. I could have taken offence at this but I am now well versed in forgiveness.

Afternoon; arranged for Alice to take Susannah to the pool then went on to Trev's afternoon seminar in the chapel, made encouraging sounds about his talk despite only four people turning up, collected Michael at the fairground, returned to Z19 to prepare evening meal. By this stage hips were genuinely collapsing. Wished someone would lay hands on *me* at the evening celebration so I could fall to the floor and lie down for a moment or two. Exhausted!

Thursday 10th April

Repeated yesterday's procedure in the driving rain and wind. Couldn't stay in the chalet with a good book and the electric fire on because of being a Christian VIP and being expected to turn out. Temperatures polar. We have five thick sweaters between six of us. Sun emerged for three minutes sixteen seconds precisely.

Very difficult to make seminar choices today; it's the usual banquet of super-spiritual food. Decided on 'How to Pray Together as a Couple' but had to go on my own. This was not very satisfactory. Ended up doing a role play double act with me taking both parts; felt a bit conspicuous – and alone.

Saw the same counsellor eyeing me dubiously in the Team lounge. Think he was looking for some bouncers to remove me as persona non grata. Tried to make my way towards him to explain things but he kept evading me and hiding behind tea urns, groups of chairs and Dave Pope. Eventually cornered him and tried to tell him that I was walking *to* Trev not *from* him, that the Christian walk was a joke, at least not literally a joke but I was joking about it and that in general my hips were OK, apart of course from being a little larger than I'd like, but that they did not need the laying on of hands, just the laying off of cream. He did not laugh; in fact I get the impression that he thinks I am some kind of dangerous lunatic, sent to Spring Onion to deceive him.

What possessed me to talk about my hip size to a complete stranger?

Friday 11th April

There is now a muddy moat around the front door, though I believe this was formed during the night from defrosting puddles and melting icicles. 5,000 people, including me, are petitioning God for a break in the rain and those who operate in faith ministries are believing for a heat wave. What happened to the 'two or three agreeing on anything' principle? Have we all got it wrong? Or are there *more* than 5,000 Christians somewhere else praying for torrential rain over the UK? On reflection this seems unlikely. Does God work according to a majority anyhow? Maybe satanists are trying to destroy Spring Onion. Need to discern God's will about the weather and then pray. At my usual speed of discerning God's will, Spring Onion will be over by about a month before I've decided which way to pray.

Abandoned Trev's seminar to go to the nearest town and buy two more umbrellas and another sweater. Stood against the evil forces, exercised faith and bought sunglasses too. This was very difficult to explain to Susannah and Michael.

Felt obliged to step out in a dramatic act of faith and wore them to Trev's major seminar on 'Signs and Wonders'. Did take an umbrella and a sweater as well since it was still overcast and raining heavily. Michael and Susannah refused to walk with me with my sunglasses on. Unfortunately, as I was exhorting them to hold my hands I walked right into the same zealous counsellor again. He suggested that a white stick is more dependable than children, who really should be allowed to play rather than having to act as guides to a needy parent and that I should go immediately to the seminar on 'Signs and Wonders' to receive the laying on of hands for the recovery of my sight as well as a miracle for my hips. Unfortunately he insisted on accompanying me there. Clearly, he doesn't know I'm Trev's wife. Hid in the back row and tried to make my escape several times. Some men just won't listen when they've already made their minds up. They have an inbuilt assumption that 'No' means 'Yes' and all we need is a little encouragement. Mounting horror. At the end he pushed me forward for ministry which I did not need, from a person I know is not into ministry (yet). Had a rising feeling that I was about to be hailed as an example of miraculous healing and later unmasked as a deceiver, planted by Trev to dupe the congregation. Prayed that none of *our* congregation would be there. Stood helplessly at the front feeling an all-time nerd. Just at the last moment

I noticed the side exit sign and edged my way towards it. Made my escape and ran like the clappers back to Z19.

Hadn't focused on a word Trev said but assured him that he had been wonderful.

Amazingly victorious, exciting, challenging evening celebration; really felt like part of a mighty army. Wish all of the Christian life could be like Spring Onion celebrations.

Saturday 12th April

Avoided the main morning Bible reading for obvious reasons.

Evening celebration great. So many people came forward that extra counsellors were needed.

My big chance to lay hands on someone at last.

I am disgusted. Alice and Tim had them falling like flies, Trev's were resting on the floor and grinning all over their faces but all I got was someone with an intimate female problem.

Prayed for one or two others who stood rooted to the spot. Felt nothing but failure and embarrassment, but had to reassure them that God was still blessing them even if it was a vertical blessing. Not sure if I believed this myself. Felt I'd really let them down. Wish it had been literally.

Worse to come. Stood at the front, surrounded by bodies – none of them my doing, when I felt the dreaded hands of the hyper-active counsellor land on my shoulders. Fell to the floor faster than you can say

'Kansas City Prophets'. Though the fall was totally self-imposed, I did feel a real peace envelop me. My body relaxed and I do believe I even drifted into sleep. Hard to say whether this was the result of exhaustion or something more spiritual.

Sunday 13th April

Final communion service. It's hard to express love to God when you're in the middle of a process of self-analysis and so aware of your own failure. I wanted to be a shining star not a spent match, the dispenser of nourishment not the receiver. Everybody else was in one of those end of conference up-moods: all rejoicing, well fed spiritually and at peace. I felt like my inside was full of wet cotton wool. Surreptitiously checked my diary to see if I could blame PMS for how I feel; claim invalid. Nearly didn't take communion until I'd sorted out where I was spiritually and whether I qualified as a VIP or a pleb, then remembered that VIPs are just plebs in disguise and that communion is for people like me: failures who've nobody else to blame and who haven't quite made it yet. Imprinted the words 'I'm accepted, I'm forgiven' on my brain. Felt better. Then reminded myself that God had definitely used Trev, and I had been on his back-up team providing food, encouragement, umbrellas and cups of tea. I think there should be a verse that says, 'Blessed are the tea-makers, for you will fill their cup to over-flowing.'

Monday 14th April

Got too busy last week at Spring Onion to stop and rest in the new thing God has done in me. Somehow it all got lost in activity and excitement and being a VIP. My eyes got glued back on myself again, with the usual predictable results. Trouble is I want to be a very noticed channel; acknowledged and important.

Tuesday 15th April

The children grew like weeds spiritually during Spring Onion, though I suppose this is hardly an appropriate comparison. They've seen God in action and they want more. They seem to find it easier just to take God at his word. I suppose that's what it means by becoming like little children – simply trusting, with no negotiations and not a lot of doubt as to the miracles God can do.

Wednesday 16th April

Course on finding your spiritual gift arrived in the post today. Bit late for Spring Onion. I suppose this *was* God's timing though. Sometimes I wish he would work to a more obvious time scale – one that I could understand and follow; one that felt safer and didn't have any cliff-hanging finishes, or 'you're flying solo with me' kind of feelings.

Thursday 17th April

Wonder if there's a gift of forgiveness mentioned in the spiritual gifts course? Still, whatever comes, I am going to be a jack of all trades no longer. Trouble is, I have been living in 'appropriate ministry wife reaction mode' for so long, ie, the plugging of all holes (especially those nobody else wants) and filling of all gaps ('Just temporarily of course, dear') that I don't know what is really me and what is simply a trained response. I always feel obliged to react positively to 'Oh, we thought that you should do it since you're the pastor's wife', so I no longer know what is instinct and what is learned behaviour. I'm like Pavlov's dog; conditioned to respond to all church stimuli, especially phone calls. I salivate (metaphorically) the instant the phone rings, ready to rush into action. I must learn to respond to God, not merely to people and their wishes. It's very easy to keep people happy and not please God at all.

Friday 18th April

Trev having trouble finding sermon inspiration. The tell-tale signs are always the same: a desk littered with open files, commentaries from Genesis to Revelation lying in a state of abandoned disarray, five or six separate half-pages of rejected, attempted openings next to five or six half-drunk cups of coffee and Trev making endless pastoral phone calls and reading magazine articles in a futile attempt to pretend the evil day is never coming. Why do men try to hide from the inevitable? I suggested he might helpfully write an article for those pastors who are driven to prepare the next Sunday's sermon on Monday mornings, entitled 'Ten Practical Steps to More Effective Procrastination in Sermon Writing'. Brought him another cup of coffee.

Remembered later that I should have prayed for him too. Why is my spiritual compass so out of line? Even I'm getting fed up with me.

Saturday 19th April

Trev seriously behind in sermon preparation now. By tea-time only the evening's masterpiece was anywhere near completion, then disaster struck in the shape of a friendly visit from Sam Priddle wanting to discuss whether greeters could be female as well as male. Such vital matters for fellowship life should only be brought to the pastor's attention late on a Saturday evening.

Found an excellent piece entitled 'Manuscript Preparation After Midnight When You Haven't an Idea in Your Head', and left it on his desk with a double-strength cup of coffee.

Still, the exhilaration of totally depending on God must be quite something.

Sunday 20th April

Sermon ready on time but just a little incoherent in the delivery – no doubt due to the two and a half hour's sleep the previous night.

The announcements proved to be more of a problem. Poor Trev began well but came a little unstuck. 'The church treasure hunt on Saturday 3rd May is bug-eh, bug-eh, what's the word?' Thought he'd finally cracked from the stress and Sybil Sharpe went puce. 'Bug-eh friendly, oh, yes, *buggy*-friendly.' Trev looked up in mystified innocence at the rows of amused faces. He asked us later why telling the church that the church treasure hunt was for all ages and was on paths suitable for baby buggies was so funny.

Monday 21st April

Had a worrying thought: what if my spiritual gifts as discovered in the new American course aren't the same as the 'mercy, leadership and encouragement' of a few Sundays ago at the charismatic church. Surely God won't contradict himself?

Thought about ideas for Trev's birthday present. None.

Tuesday 22nd April

Shopping for Trev's birthday present. It must be something different; Trev needs to get out of his middle-aged rut. Rejected a trendy pink dog-collar shirt, unwearable; debated a session with an image consultant, unsure; considered a book entitled 'How to Develop a Submissive and Adoring Congregation', unimaginable! Mission unsuccessful.

Wednesday 23rd April

It came to me today: I am going to make a new man of Trev.

And I'm going to let God make a new woman of me. I'm going to keep my spiritual hands open – and up!

Thursday 24th April

Committee meeting tonight to discuss the future of the Sunday evening service. The numbers attending this service are enough to fill the hall if we place the chairs in rows six feet apart and leave three feet between each chair.

I think I am the token woman on this committee. This is a new role. Normally I am not on any committee since Trev is usually on all committees already and my views are assumed to be the same as his; little do they know! Since I am representative of all women I must speak particularly carefully. My comments must be wise and weighty, gracious and perceptive. I must not fill empty space with sound but not be so quiet as to be deemed a non-contributor. A lot hangs on the token woman.

Friday 25th April

Trev's birthday. Bundled him into the car and took him to his secret birthday event: his first session at the gym with an introductory assessment and personal training plan from the resident expert. I am not sure if 'enthusiasm' was quite the right word to describe his response. I am sure he will thank me for it eventually.

He wonders why Pris Priddle bought him a dictionary and underlined the word 'stroller' in red pen.

Trev suffering from lower back pain and lower still self-esteem. Apparently none of the other men at the gym wore black lycra leggings and a neatly tucked-in striped T-shirt.

Saturday 26th April

Bought a ready-made cake for Sunday night's fellowship time, on the principle that I am divesting myself of all previous assumptions about myself. I am now no longer obliged to be a home-baker. As far as I am concerned, if Sarah Lee or Mr Kipling can do it better, then let them!

Sunday 27th April

Why did Trev preach on 'Bodily exercise profits a little'? Felt hurt and just a little got at.

Monday 28th April

Day off. Trev has no idea about calories and their unfortunate after-effects. He actually thinks a cheese sandwich is virtuous and mayonnaise a divine invention. It's not so much *what* he weighs but where it has all gathered together.

Tuesday 29th April

Talked to Trev about spiritual gifts and the Holy Spirit. More agreement here than over the calories.

Disgusted. Thought Trev was so much more spiritual than me. Left him praying in the kitchen at midnight and came down at 1 am to find him eating all the fridge left-overs. Think this is called a night of prayer and feasting.

Wednesday 30th April

Sybil Sharpe's daughter, Lois Eunice Sheba (queen of), phoned to arrange a 'little chat' with me. She wouldn't say what it was about. This kind of phone call always worries me.

Received another church phone call of the 'just sharing it for prayer' variety. Apparently Wesley Tweed was seen holding a suspiciously bottle-shaped package, wearing a balaclava and talking to Lois Eunice Sheba outside the off licence. I'm not sure if I'm expected to pray for a liason between Sheba and Wesley, against the off licence or that the contents of all bottle-shaped packages should be revealed. Phoned Mitzi. Just to share this dilemma for prayer.

Thursday 1st May

Pris phoned tonight to say she was getting reports that the pastor had been seen wearing black lycra leggings and a balaclava, carrying a large black sports bag and a bottle and talking to Sheba Sharpe in the off licence. He was, according to some sources, glowing with sweat and looked exhausted. Some thought he must have run all the way from home. A number of people were 'just sharing it for prayer'.

We don't need to start an official prayer chain in this church, we have one already; it's called the gossip chat line.

Had a very wicked thought. Could phone susceptible church members and say, 'I think Sybil Sharpe looks ill, she's a very bad colour, looks as if it might be her liver.' That would be sure to 'just share its way for prayer' into 'Sybil Sharpe is a very bad mother and an awful giver' or perhaps into 'Sybil Sharpe is seriously ill. She's a very bad colour and we've heard it might be cirrhosis of the liver' and thence into 'Sybil Sharpe has been drinking secretly and now she's got cirrhosis of the liver'. The possibilities are endless.

Friday 2nd May

Lois Eunice Sheba (queen of) came round. Took a brave step and asked if I could just call her Sheba. She has given me permission as long as I add the 'queen of' bit.

Apparently she feels called to go to the Falkland

Islands. She has seen an advertisement in the Christian press asking for female workers for the troops stationed there. I must say I think this wording just a little unfortunate. Sheba says she is willing to endure men, tropical heat and creepy crawlies for the Lord, none of which she apparently likes. That's how she knows it is 'of the Lord'. The frequent occurrence of the word 'men' in her recent Bible readings has also confirmed her sacrificial calling. Her mother thinks she would collect many trophies of grace for the Lord there. She was most taken aback when I told her that the Falkland Islands were, to my knowledge, colder than here and did not specialise in creepy crawlies. Though I thought there were probably quite a lot of men. She is going to check her calling and see if the Lord meant The Maldives or some other needy place where she can sacrifice herself for God in tropical, men-infested climes. She was concerned though that large numbers of men in the Falklands would have to do without her. Almost asked her if Wesley had been called too.

Saturday 3rd May

Church Treasure Hunt today. Why are otherwise normally civilised church members so competitive when it comes to their children? Despite oceans of mud it was a nail-biting double buggy race to the finish with mud-spattered toddlers and children. Frenzied fathers fought their way through the rain, which, in my experience, dogs most outdoor Christian events.

Could have done with the Maclaren team to unclog the chariot wheels in a pit stop.

Sunday 4th May

Family service morning. This really means children's service morning. Trev had diligently collected an array of large cardboard boxes from sundry sources, some rolls of heavy duty tape and a few staple guns. He invited the dads in the congregation to construct an extra-large model of Noah's Ark from these and then the children were all to go inside and make appropriate animal sounds, after which he would deliver a thought-provoking message on God's provision. This was not a good idea. It's amazing how macho men feel about constructing things – maybe it's the primitive home-building instinct. Hordes of avid do-it-yourselfers swarmed round the front constructing a double-decker of warship proportions. The children got so hyped up that it sounded like all the inhabitants of London Zoo had escaped and were having a drunken party at the front of our church.

Trev's training did not include crowd control. Once inside, the animals had a wonderful time and insisted in roaming about the ark quite freely during the ensuing talk, intermittently giving out trumpeting, bellowing, roaring and other indescribable animal sounds from the furthest corners of the construction. Trev singularly failed to make himself heard over the cacophony. Maybe Noah had similar problems. The Bible story pictures suggest such co-operation and order though. Communion, which followed, was peppered by the sounds of a very small rogue elephant who could not be dislodged from the inner reaches of the ark and who bit every time a hand was reached in for him.

It was also particularly unfortunate that the upper living quarters for Noah and his wife had been constructed from a Bell's whisky box.

Overheard Sybil Sharpe's exocet missile finding its target at the end of the service: 'How could you, Pastor? How dare you! To use an advertisement for such a beverage in the construction of Noah's Ark is beyond belief.'

Monday 5th May

Managed to find time to look at the spiritual gifts course today. It is all very carefully set out with teaching notes and timings and illustrations and videos and bits to fill in. I think Americans do things this way – very professionally. (It is possible to call this 'slick' if one is feeling trans-Atlantically threatened.) We seem to muddle through with hand-written OHP slides, illegible hand-outs and no idea of accurate finishing times. We do, however, always allow time for tea.

Trev and I filled in the appropriate questionnaires on each other. Trev was very glad to discover that he has preaching and pastoral gifts. I was hoping that maybe he would have been a secret administrator or leader so he could stop being a pastor and become a successful businessman. This was a very unspiritual thought. We could, of course, have gone on being committed to the church but be able to retreat when things got troublesome in church life and not get hurt anymore. Afraid to look at my own 'spiritual gift profile' – as the course calls it. Delayed it as long as I could. I can't believe it! God was right, or rather the charismatic pastor heard him right. I do have gifts of mercy, leadership and encouragement. Thank you, Lord.

I would also like the gift of hearing God clearly. I think I will ask for this. If this is the gift of discernment, I will earnestly covet it. This would be a good thing to do. Prayed tonight, 'Dear Lord, please give me hearing ears, wide open, big ears, so I don't miss your voice. In Jesus' name, Amen.'

Tuesday 6th May

Evening service committee coming up again. How does one appear wise without looking old? I want to look like the kind of woman who dispenses gems of mature, inspired truth without looking wizened, wrinkly and grey; I would like the Jill Briscoe look – international woman of purpose, wise but with a touch of humour. I could try no make-up; women whose skin glows with scrubbed health are assumed to be very spiritual. Tried an American Christian magazine for inspiration. I notice the dowdy, spiritual look does not seem to apply there. There they all look like models with flawless skin. They also seem to have some kind of speakers' uniform – a tailored jacket, a carefully placed piece of jewellery on the lapel and a warm, confident smile.

Wednesday 7th May

Bought a jacket and tried to throw out my cardigan. Made three trips to the bin but couldn't do it: a) It would be a waste, b) I'm attached to it, and c) I might need it again if I fail as a power-dresser. Pinned Susannah's Wallace and Gromit brooch to my jacket lapel.

Thursday 8th May

My reputation as a thoughtful and wise token woman committee member is gone, despite the smart navy jacket and the brooch. I had only mentally drifted away for a moment, and I think I must have subconsciously heard the chairman's despairing, rhetorical question, 'What shall we do with the evening service?' but it seems I was heard humming the tune of 'What shall we do with the drunken sailor?' while a most significant spiritual point about reaching the lost was being made.

Friday 9th May

Susannah wants us to buy a lottery ticket. 'Just once, Mum. It only costs a pound and I'm the only one in our class who hasn't ever done it.' The tried and tested technique, exercised by children everywhere, of wearing the parent down and inducing copious quantities of guilt.

I have told her that Christians do not buy lottery tickets. Her understanding of Christian decision-making may be a little blurred by the fact that Michael has made it his habit to run out into the street every Saturday evening after the lottery draw is made, shouting out to all and sundry at the top of his voice, 'We've won! We've won! Hooray!' and other appropriate but untrue celebratory remarks. I imagine the neighbours have cottoned onto the fact that we could not possibly have won every single week, though well-meaning and gullible passers-by have been known to congratulate him. He needs taking in hand.

Saturday 10th May

Succumbed to Susannah's prolonged siege attack re. the purchase of a lottery ticket. This had to be a carefully planned event requiring fine-tuned tactics.

First precaution: phoned the SS and put the phone down without speaking, to check that she was safely at home and not out shopping, potentially in the vicinity of a lottery sales point.

Second precaution: threatened Susannah with dire consequences if she should ever tell anyone what we were about to do.

Third precaution: drove a long way from home to a totally remote area.

Fourth precaution: chose a supermarket as my purchasing point.

Fifth precaution: had a fully laden supermarket trolley beside us, so if the worst came to the worst we could pretend to be just passing the lottery stand.

Sixth precaution: didn't tell Trev.

Seventh precaution: prayed most earnestly that we would win nothing.

Had never had a lottery ticket in my hand before and was not quite sure how to fill it in. Susannah did not seem to have the same problem.

Muttered under my breath, 'Lord, please don't let us win anything. Please just direct us to choose all the wrong numbers, for your glory and good name, and for our good name too, Lord. Please don't let any of these numbers come up, not even as a bonus ball, whatever that is.' The lady next to me edged away from us as if we were a pair of axe-wielding psychopaths, but could see her trying to read our ticket out of the corner of her eye.

Eventually she asked, 'Do you have contact with some sort of deity?' When I said, 'Yes, the Lord God himself,' she asked if I was sure I could trust him. 'Of course,' I said, 'He is totally dependable and abundantly reliable.' In that case could we tell her which numbers he'd told us to choose so as not to win, so she could eliminate them. And would he be able to tell her which numbers to choose in order to win, and if possible could I ask him for her. How do I get myself into these impossible situations? I could see she was most confused when I said God wasn't the least interested in lottery tickets, but only in the certainties of life like heaven and hell. At this point she fled. Does this count as witnessing?

Trev couldn't understand my eager desire to watch the lottery draw. Hung on Mystic Meg's every word. Think this is probably sinful. Nearly fainted when she said she saw a name beginning with L and a house with lots of children. Knelt before the TV in desperation, in a last-minute bid for clemency, petitioning the Lord to avoid 12, 29, 36, 17, 40, 25 and especially 42. 'Lord, I will never, never, ever do the lottery again. I will give all my money away to the poor. I will never say anything negative about anyone in our church.' Watched the little balls run down the slope, in terror, still begging God to let them be all wrong.

Thank you, God! You are a God who answers prayer. I will trust you always.

Prayer warfare is exhausting.

Sunday 11th May

What are things coming to? Trev was innocently announcing a forthcoming, most serious and relevant conference for men on the topic 'Money, Sex and Power' when an anonymous male voice from the back shouted out, 'Are those *all* guaranteed?'

Sometimes I am quite taken aback by Christian men.

Monday 12th May

Trev cut the grass today. A mistake. Six church members slowed down and called from their cars, 'Great to have time off when the rest of us have to work!' or 'Must be wonderful to have to work only one day a week!' All church members who express such opinions should be obliged to prepare the next Sunday's sermons, preach them, produce a set of home Bible study notes, counsel a serious depressive and deal with the follow-up phone calls, prepare an elders' meeting agenda, conduct the elders' meeting, visit a few senior citizens, do a day's administration, answer twenty or so phone calls on a wide variety of topics, make ten more phone calls on church and denominational matters, speak at a school SU meeting and prepare for it, chair at least one difficult committee meeting, strategise for the coming months, pray for the congregation and only have time for a few hours off that week.

Obviously pastors should only cut their grass at dead of night when no church members could possibly see them, or perhaps Sunday afternoon would be better.

Tuesday 13th May

The old, 'I am hard done by', negative feeling is coming back again. The bane of all ministry wives. Need an injection of truth and vigorous faith. Where has the Spirit gone? Sometimes I seem to lose him!

Wednesday 14th May

Mid-week prayer meeting. Strong 'um' level this week – most encouraging. There's nothing like a generous muttering of 'ums' to encourage one in public prayer. In fact, praying into stony silence can be quite unnerving. There seems to be an unspoken 'um rating' for agreement in prayer. Two or three 'ums' every paragraph or two and you know you're on the right track. If some enthusiast says, 'Um, yes!' or 'Um, yes Lord!' then you're on a real winner. An 'Amen' in the middle of a prayer or better still a 'Hallelujah' and you're a super-saint mega pray-er and the Spirit is really leading you. You can pray for quite a while, even to the point of discouragement, before you get a real chorus of 'ums' going, then once you've hit the right topic you can stay there for a while. It's like getting a round of applause. You can say to yourself with certainty, 'Wow, I'm really in touch with the one or two here.' I'm not sure if this is the same thing as being really in touch with God though. Very tempted to follow the 'ums' tonight. Sounded like a field of contented Friesians at one stage.

Praying for radical things, like confession and asking God to purify us gets a very faint 'um' response, but that's OK as long as it's the really spiritually minded people who are 'uming'. Prayed for the Holy Spirit to come and touch us – high 'um' response – but had to go on to pray that the Lord would deal with sin, our sin; 'ums' sounded so feeble they could have been signals from a distant galaxy. Prayed on anyhow. Want to be real with God and have my sin dealt with (privately though).

Thursday 15th May

I am getting stuck in my image rut again. Spotted the very thing I'd had in mind to dispel the ministry wife impression – the brightest, yellowest dungarees imaginable. Came home in triumph, with my old clothes in a bag and wearing my new symbol of self-expression; feeling wonderful, youthful and free from ministerial conformity. Tim spoiled it all. He called out, 'Watch out, Dad, here's banana woman.' I think children must prefer safe, conforming mothers.

Friday 16th May

Specially convened deacons' meeting to road-test several types of new chair for the sanctuary. Trev thought they could save time by testing and choosing a much-needed new Communion wine at the same time. The idea was that they would sit on the chairs while they tasted the various wines, changing chairs every half hour or so, a few minutes' sitting time being deemed inadequate for proper assessment of 'doze through sermon' potential.

They got a bit carried away with the wine; Dave thought number one had just a hint of peach with subtle undertones of radish, number two was mouthwash fresh and number three was clove rock with essence of Turkish Delight. Trev was more than a little concerned that Sam Priddle saw some similarity between number four and real ale, and that he had six refills, 'Mug size, please. Just to be sure.' How does he know what real ale tastes like? And do we want the congregation to experience real ale during Communion? Trev vetoed number four on the grounds that it provided an unspiritual experience. By this stage there were so many bottles on the table that it looked as if they were in the middle of a drunken orgy, and had got into a very slow and stupefied version of musical chairs. Sam declared chair number three to be 'Perfect for an extra-long sermon with sub-points, extended praise session followed by open prayer and a time of ministry'. He dropped off in it most contentedly and snored through the rest of the evening. It did not matter that no one else could try it, since Trev had immediately eliminated it. The whole event was like a rerun of Goldilocks and the Three Bears.

Saturday 17th May

Children's church tomorrow. Theme: 'Choose you this day whom you will serve.' Children's church should be fun and lively. I am determined to communicate in a fresh way to the children and give them a great time. Faith must be relevant to this generation. Worked out a totally themed and co-ordinated presentation and a wonderfully varied morning full of action.

Sunday 18th May

Everything was based on the idea of 'Choice'. I'd planned to reinforce the theme with lots of activities which led on to the main spiritual thrust.

We began with a choice of biscuits; plain or choco-late. Unfortunately I had not foreseen that every child would want the chocolate ones. Thought about changing the whole theme to 'Developing a servant spirit' or 'Unselfishness'. But left Tim, Alice, Michael and Susannah in charge while I ran to the corner shop and bought more chocolate biscuits so the sound of disappointed howling from four assorted two to five year olds would not filter into the service. By the time I'd got back, three sets of parents had appeared, concerned about the distress calls from their offspring. Reassured them, sent them back and continued.

We began with a noisy, total involvement activ-ity: the singing of 'The Grand Old Duke of York'; designed to teach the importance of not staying half way up, on middle ground, but making a defi-nite choice for Jesus. We had great fun with this, enthusiastically marching up and down and yelling.

> And when they were up they were up,
> And when they were down they were down,
> And when they were only half way up
> They were neither up nor down.

Had a brilliant, last-minute thought and gave them the church teapot lids to bang together as they marched. The kids loved it.

Then we moved on to an appropriately spiritual-ised version of the game 'Rats and Rabbits'. In this new improved version the children had to wait for me to call either 'Jeremiah' or 'Jehoshaphat' and run to the appropriately labelled side of the hall. Perhaps this was too advanced for them. They seemed to be incapable of remembering which side was which and some very little ones even ran to the unlabelled ends of the hall. Though perhaps, on reflection, this was to avoid being trampled to death in the middle. The twenty-five-strong flailing rugby scrum mêlée in the middle did result in slight injury to two of the more aggressive, elbowing males and one little girl who, most unfortunately, was a visting child. Nothing that a plaster and a second chocolate biscuit wouldn't fix though.

I was yelling 'Jehoshaphat' at the top of my voice when we had a pastoral visit from one of our deacons. Evidently the singing of 'Be still for the presence of the Lord, the Holy One is here' had been adversely affected by the words of 'The Grand Old Duke of York', and the sounds of a mighty army marching and banging teapot lids had done little to add to the quiet spirit of worship. Now Trev's sermon was being interrupted. Apparently the answer to his rhetorical question, 'Who must we totally depend on in times of distress?' was answered from above with a thunderous cry of 'Jeshoshaphat!'

Unfortunately, because of the delays and interruptions, we didn't quite get as far as the spiritual thrust. Got a few very disapproving looks as I crept my way out through the church.

Yet another area of significant spiritual failure.

Could see Grace looking at me but managed to avoid her.

Monday 19th May

Grace phoned and invited me for tea on Wednesday. She wants to talk to me. Since she has the gift of knowledge she probably knows about all my mistakes.

Tuesday 20th May

Are we making any spiritual progress at all? Women's Bible study group meeting on 'Heaven' tonight. Daisy Mild wanted to know if we'd all sit around there doing nothing or if we'd have humble, little jobs to do, like cleaning the toilets while God sat on the throne. Don't think she'd the slightest idea what she'd said. Innocence is a lovely quality.

Wednesday 21st May

Tea with Grace tonight. She fed me a wonderful tea then sat me in a comfy chair and just let me talk. Confided in her how miserably inept a pastor's wife I am, and in fact how miserably inept a Christian I am too, and how much of a hypocrite I feel. Found myself telling her what a failure I feel, and how hard I'm trying, and how I don't seem to be anybody's idea of a good ministry wife.

'You'd think I'd be better at it by now, after all I've had long years of practice. But I can't cook like Pris, I'm not trendy like Mitzi, I can't counsel like Mavis and I get all tied up when I worship. Half the time I'm afraid of the congregation and what they think of me. When I try to visit, I sit on the edge of the sofa in a state of nervous tension wondering what I'm going to say next. When it's my turn in the creche, mothers keep their kids at home for fear of injury. Last time I was on the flower rota the whole arrangement tilted towards the congregation so much that it looked like nuclear warheads poised for firing, and I'd used so much green sticky tape to anchor the vase to the stand that they had to take wooden stand and all to old Mrs Plum in hospital. Apparently it was the first time they'd had to put a warning sign on a patient's flowers. What can I do? I've tried to do everything right for so long. I want to be the best I can be, but I daren't let them know how unspiritual I really am. I have wrong thoughts and wrong motives and I get in a mess. And I keep losing the Holy Spirit.'

Grace handed me a poster. 'This is for you,' she said. It had a little girl on a swing, hair flying, going really high. But the swing was held at the top by a huge, strong hand, the Father's hand. 'Has it ever occurred to you that God is holding you safe and that you are his loved little girl. He's not looking for performance or success, just love and trust. Now I want you to tell *him* how you feel and then I'm going to ask him to speak to you.'

When I protested that that kind of thing didn't happen to me, she said that was OK but she'd pray anyway. I've never been prayed for like that before. She asked the Lord to come and minister to me. By the power of his Spirit to heal my wounded heart and speak whatever I needed to hear. He didn't speak. He actually came instead and hugged me. I have never felt so safe before. All I could say was, 'Thank you, Lord.'

OTHER CHRISTINA PRESS TITLES

Precious to God
Sarah Bowen   £5.99 in UK

Two young people, delighted to be starting a family, have their expectations shattered by the arrival of a handicapped child. And yet this is only the first of many difficulties to be faced. What was initially a tragedy, is through faith, transformed into a story of inspiration, hope and spiritual enrichment.

'I was deeply moved by Sarah's story. Do read it.'
Celia Bowring

Angels Keep Watch
Carol Hathorne   £5.99 in UK

A true adventure showing how God still directs our lives, not with wind, earthquake or fire, but by the still small voice.

'Go to Africa.' The Lord had been saying it for over forty years. At last, Carol Hathorne had obeyed, going out to Kenya with her husband. On the eastern side of Nairobi, where tourists never go, they came face to face with dangers, hardship and poverty on a daily basis, but experienced the joy of learning that Christianity is still growing in God's world.

Carol Hathorne is an Anglican priest working in a parish near Dudley, West Midlands. Her husband, Mark, is a Methodist minister in the same area.